MODERN VEGETARIAN
Instant Pot®
COOKBOOK

OFFICIAL
Instant Pot
BOOK

MODERN VEGETARIAN
Instant Pot®
COOKBOOK

101 veggie and vegan recipes for your multi-cooker

JENNY TSCHIESCHE
PHOTOGRAPHY BY CLARE WINFIELD

OFFICIAL
Instant Pot
BOOK

RYLAND PETERS & SMALL
LONDON • NEW YORK

Art director Leslie Harrington
Editorial director Julia Charles
Head of production Patricia Harrington
Publisher Cindy Richards

Prop stylist Olivia Wardle
Food stylist Emily Kydd
Assistant food stylist Katy Gilhooly
Indexer Hilary Bird

First published in 2021 by
Ryland Peters & Small
20–21 Jockey's Fields
London WC1R 4BW
and 341 E 116th St
New York NY 10029
www.rylandpeters.com

10 9 8 7 6 5 4 3 2 1

Text © Jenny Tschiesche 2021
Design and photographs © Ryland Peters & Small 2021

INSTANT POT® and associated logos are owned by Instant Brands Inc. and are used under license. Visit www.instantpot.co.uk or www.instantpot.com for more detailed information on Instant Pot® products and their usage.

ISBN: 978-1-78879-344-5

A CIP record for this book is available from the British Library. US Library of Congress Cataloging-in-Publication Data has been applied for.

Printed in China

Disclaimer:
The views expressed in this book are those of the author but they are general views only. Ryland Peters & Small hereby exclude all liability to the extent permitted by law for any errors or omissions in this book and for any loss, damage or expense (whether direct or indirect) suffered by a third party relying on any information contained in this book.

General Notes:
• Note that the 6-litre/quart Instant Pot Duo Plus™ and the Instant Pot Duo Evo™ Plus 10-in-1 Multi Pressure Cooker models of multi-cooker were used for devising and testing the recipes featured in this book, and preparing them for the photography featured. If you are using an alternative brand of multi-cooker please refer closely to the specific manufacturer's manual in order to adjust the operating instructions as appropriate for each recipe.

• Both British (Metric) and American (Imperial oz. plus cup) measurements are included in these recipes for your convenience. Work with one set of measurements only and not alternate between the two within a recipe.

• All spoon measurements are level unless otherwise specified: 1 tsp = 5 ml, 1 tbsp = 15 ml

• Recipes marked with a 'V' are suitable for vegans, or can be easily adapted to suit a vegan diet.

• Please note that in this book the term 'legumes' is used to refer to all foods in the legume family and as such includes beans, lentils and peas (including split peas and chickpeas) i.e. foods more commonly referred to as 'pulses' in the UK and 'legumes' in the US, and also includes peanuts.

• Some cheeses (such as traditional Parmesan) are made using animal rennet. Check packaging carefully to ensure the cheese you are using is made with a microbial starter and suitable for a vegetarian diet.

• All eggs used are large (UK)/ extra-large (US) unless specified otherwise. Uncooked or partially cooked eggs should not be served to the elderly, frail, young children, pregnant women or those with compromised immune systems.

Useful Terminology Used in Recipes:
QPR: Quick Pressure Release literally means you manually release the pressure quickly by opening the vent valve on the top of the machine to open. Take care to make sure the vent is not going to expel steam straight onto a socket or any electrical equipment.

NPR: Natural Pressure Release refers to allowing the pot to release built-up pressure naturally. You'll know when it's done because the pressure button will pop back down. Some recipes call for a period of NPR before QPR. This means allowing the specified time after cooking (for NPR) before you release any residual pressure (QPR).

PIP: Pot In Pot means cooking foods in a pot inside your Instant Pot®. This can be used to make porridge, frittatas and cakes.

Inner Pot: This is the stainless steel pot that you do all your cooking in. It's durable and easily washed. I tend to wash, dry and immediately replace the pot so I don't have any mishaps. People have been known to pour water straight into the pot with no inner pot there – that's a quick way to ruin your Instant Pot®.

CONTENTS

Foreword **6**

Introduction **8**

Porridges & Dhals **12**

Soups & Stews **26**

Curries & Chillies **42**

Rice & Quinoa **64**

Pasta **82**

Eggs & Cheese **92**

Side Dishes **106**

Sweet Things & Drinks **122**

Index **142**

Acknowledgements **144**

FOREWORD
BY LEON TAYLOR, OLYMPIAN

As a former Olympic diver, I am very aware of the connection between food and wellbeing. Working with Jenny over several years has shown me how passionate she is about that connection too. She and I first met in the company of royalty over seven years ago. We were both working for a charity called SportsAid and I had been tasked with introducing HRH The Duchess of Cambridge, the patron of SportsAid, to future GB Athletes whilst Jenny was running nutrition workshops for the athletes with HRH in attendance. Quite a way to be introduced to someone! What I realised that day is that Jenny has a knack of translating nutrition facts into delicious recipes which I have been lucky enough to taste at her sports nutrition demos over the years.

Ironically, I began focusing more on my diet after my Olympic success when I realised that a balance between exercise, mindfulness and nutrition needs to be sought. For many years I have followed a predominantly plant-based diet. This way of eating has helped me to achieve the balance that I want in terms of energy, sleep, digestive health, mental health and overall health and wellbeing. It is a way of eating that seems also to suit some of the areas in the world where populations live the longest. These areas known as 'The Blue Zones' are where a significant number of centenarians live. The secret to their longevity seems to lie in their adherence to a balanced life that incorporates some relaxation, exercise and a seasonal and predominantly vegetarian diet.

When Jenny started talking about a kitchen appliance called an Instant Pot® I was intrigued. I know she is keen to make recipes simple for those following them and now this book has come along, and I cannot tell you how excited I am to start using Jenny's recipes. The Instant Pot® is so well suited to plant-based and vegetarian eating. Whether it is bulk cooking protein-rich legumes such as beans, peas and lentils in next to no time, or the ability to make the most delicious nutrient-rich dahls, soups, stews and risottos with ease and speed, this appliance makes

these meals absolute dinner winners for busy people. The appeal of preparing meals this way is clear – from creating dinner party feasts to meal-prepping for a busy week ahead, this style of cooking just works.

When I moved to eating a more plant-based diet I researched how to make the best and most nutritious choices but with this book you don't need to do your own research. Jenny is a skilled and experienced nutrition expert with an ability to translate theory into practical, simple and delicious recipes. Whether you are looking for a new way to enjoy the wonderful texture of quinoa, chickpeas or lentils, in a quinotto, stew or curry or you simply want a creamy sweet or savoury porridge that cooks whilst you're in the shower in the mornings this is a way of cooking that will suit both your lifestyle and your nutritional needs. We all live in a busy world and few of us have time to cook from scratch, but if cooking from scratch takes less time than ordering a takeaway or standing in line at your local on-the-go food stop it's got to be a better option, right?

In my role now as a speaker, executive coach and mentor I have mentored many young athletes, coached many high-performance executives and spoken in front of thousands of people. It is clear to me that in order to achieve amazing results you have to invest time and energy in looking after yourself. Eating well, sleeping well, moving well and relaxing well are all very much part of a more balanced approach to achieving the best version of ourselves. I encourage people not to get het up about eating the 'wrong food' or missing a day of exercise. However, when they can focus on adding positive elements into their lives that become normal and second nature, that's when they start to get results. Making delicious, nutritious meals in minutes is part of the whole process. You may not love cooking, but you should love yourself and your body. Nourishing your body with these vegetarian and vegan meals, made simply and easily using the Instant Pot®, is a great way to care for your body and achieve the balance you are looking for.

INTRODUCTION

After the success of my first Instant Pot® cookery book I found numerous people wanting a vegetarian and vegan version. It was very common for me to be asked how many of the recipes in the first book were vegetarian or vegan. I had the numbers at the tip of my tongue, so, in response I felt I had to produce a WHOLE book of vegetarian and vegan recipes.

As a nutrition expert and health writer with a busy schedule I know how important it is for recipes to be simple and easy to follow, and that they do not contain too many complicated ingredients. That's where this book excels. It's a compilation of delicious and nutritious, but importantly, simple-to-follow dishes that are either vegetarian or vegan or both!

This book has been created for those people who simply want to incorporate more vegetarian and vegan meals into their lives whether for health, environmental, budget or other reasons. If health is your primary concern, then looking to the places in the world where vegetarian eating is very much a part of the culture is helpful. Alongside fewer cases of diabetes, cancer and heart-related illness, these parts of the world also have lower rates for depression and other mental health issues. Here they eat more vegetables (a great source of fibre and many vitamins and minerals), more legumes, including beans, peas, lentils and chickpeas (which are all rich in fibre and protein), more wholegrains (which are also rich in fibre) and more nuts and seeds (also sources of fibre, protein and polyunsaturated and monounsaturated fats).

If you are wanting to save money, then this way of eating really does keep the costs low. Canned or dried legumes (lentils, chickpeas, beans), for example, are very cost effective. Some of the most nutritious dishes can be made on a shoestring budget. Not only are these foods economical they also take on whatever flavours you want, be that Italian, Spanish, Mexican or Indian. This makes them incredibly versatile and therefore you can use them in multiple dishes.

Frozen and wonky vegetables are no less nutritious and can also save you a lot of money. Buying frozen vegetables when they would not otherwise be in season is beneficial from a nutrient perspective. Furthermore, the flavour, texture, nutritional value and cost benefits of fresh fruit and vegetables in season is undeniable. These recipes were created across a year so there should be dishes that are best depending on where you are in the world in each of the seasons.

If you're looking at moving to more vegetarian and vegan dishes for sustainability reasons you may already know that by reducing the number of animal products in your diet and by buying local, sustainable produce you can help drive the local economy and reduce the reliance on factory farming which is an unsustainable way of producing food.

Vegetarian and vegan meals are a healthy way of enjoying great-tasting and nutritious food whether you're vegetarian, vegan or simply want to eat more plant-based foods. If you are thinking of moving to vegetarianism or veganism then you may have questions about achieving nutrition balance. Both macronutrients and micronutrients are available from a varied vegetarian or vegan diet, a little bit of knowledge about where these can be found can go a long way.

Fats to Cook With
Throughout this book you will notice the use of oil, butter or vegan spread. As with most things in the world of food and nutrition there will be healthier and less healthy versions available.

As far as oils go, I tend to cook with extra virgin olive oil, avocado oil or coconut oil. If the recipe calls for butter the best varieties of butter will be those made from the milk of grass-fed or organic cows. Better vegan spreads are those that are fortified, especially those fortified with vitamins D and B12, those made with vegetable oils (no GM ingredients and no hydrogenated oils) and coloured naturally too (typically with carotenes). They must be suitable for cooking with as you're looking for texture and flavour similar to butter.

Sugars

In the previous book I specified certain sugars for recipes but in this book I have left that largely to you. I prefer coconut sugar to be used in Asian (Thai and Indonesian) dishes for flavour reasons but it really is up to you.

As a nutritionist I would always recommend less refined sugars as they have more nutrients left in. Rapadura would be my number one choice but that's not that easy to come by and can be costly to buy. From rapadura to refined white sugar there are many sugars in between that are more or less refined. Try and buy as unrefined as your budget and logistics will allow.

Soaking Legumes

Beans, lentils, peas and nuts have a lot going for them nutritionally. They're a source of iron, complex carbohydrates, starches, fibre and in the case of nuts and seeds, also a good source of fats. These are a healthy part of a balanced vegetarian diet.

However, if you have started to increase your consumption of these foods you may have noticed some unwanted side effects. Many people will suffer from excess gas and wind. However, this can also be significantly reduced or even eliminated by soaking first. This is a step carried out in traditional cultures for centuries where beans, lentils and peas form a large part of the diet. It is the initial step prior to sprouting and serves the purpose of reducing the amount of phytic acid in the beans, lentils and peas, reducing the tannins whilst making them more digestible and the nutrients iron, zinc and calcium easier to absorb.

Pressure cooking legumes whether pre-soaked or not makes for a quick and budget-friendly way of producing a fantastic and nutritious vegetarian and vegan protein. In fact, pressure cookers are common in many Indian households, which is a predominantly vegetarian culture, for this very reason.

Grains

Whilst wholegrains are a source of fibre and therefore release energy more slowly into the body, I also use risotto rice and basmati rice (white) in some of my recipes too. Where a dish is heavier in refined carbohydrates e.g. in the case of a risotto, I would recommend serving with vegetables (including those in the dish itself), or a salad to contribute fibre and micronutrients to the overall meal. Almost all other dishes contain wholegrains e.g. brown rice, quinoa, oats and/or a protein source e.g. legumes, eggs and cheese. Fibre and protein both help to balance energy levels.

Eggs and Egg Alternatives

If for health or ethical reasons you do not eat eggs, then there will be a few recipes in this book that you are unable to eat. However, where baking is concerned you can replace one egg with one of the following:

1 tbsp ground flaxseeds soaked in 3 tbsp warm water
1 tbsp chia seeds soaked in 3 tbsp water
1/2 banana, mashed
65 g/1/4 cup Apple Purée (see recipe on page 125)

Combining Proteins

One thing that those moving to more plant-based and vegetarian eating have concerns about is ensuring they are eating enough protein. Animal-based proteins are what are known as 'complete proteins' because they contain all nine of what are called 'essential amino acids' i.e. the ones you have to eat as the human body is incapable of making them. Plant-based foods are not always complete proteins. However, each plant-based food contains its own combinations of amino acids so by combining grains and pulses, nuts and pulses, dairy and grains, and nuts and grains you can create complete proteins in your meals.

Dairy and eggs are complete proteins but so are quinoa, oats and chia seeds. You will find these ingredients in this book, but also other dishes made up of incomplete proteins that could either be combined within one meal or throughout one day. It's easy to combine two incomplete protein sources to get the nutrients you need. You can combine foods to make what is called complementary proteins. Two incomplete proteins can be combined to obtain all the essential amino acids. For example, brown rice has several of the essential amino acids, but not all nine. Beans, lentils and chickpeas have essential amino acids that brown rice lacks. Simply pairing rice and beans gives you a vegan meal with complete proteins.

Cooking Pasta Dishes

Pasta Cooking Times: Use half the time stated on the packet and add 1 minute. If the time stated on the packet is an odd number, then round up not down. For example, if a packet states 9 minutes cooking time then use 5 minutes plus 1, i.e. 6 minutes in total as your cooking time. If the pasta is a little al dente then stir on KEEP WARM until it is cooked through or leave in the pot once stirred and come back in a few minutes.

Starch Release: Pasta releases starch when cooked. In a big pot of water that you are subsequently going to drain off i.e. on the hob/stovetop, starch release doesn't need much consideration. However, in Instant Pot® cooking you always need to think about what other ingredients you're using in your dish. Too many starch releasing ingredients e.g. starchy vegetables or raw legumes and the whole dish will BURN to the bottom of the pot.

With pasta dishes, once they have cooked for the specified time just allow another 30 seconds after the beeping to allow the contents to settle. Do a QPR after this time which means you're less likely to get spluttering through the SEALING VALVE.

Finally, just remember that these recipes have all been tested using exact quantities of ingredients. If you want to put your own spin on them then think about adding liquid-releasing vegetables, e.g. mushrooms, celery, pak choi, courgette/zucchini rather than sweet potato. The recipes in this book have been a joy to develop. I hope you enjoy making and eating them as much as I enjoyed creating them for you.

NUTRIENT	VEGETARIAN/VEGAN FOOD SOURCE
Protein	eggs, cheese, yogurt, legumes (beans, lentils, peas, peanuts), nuts, seeds, soy foods (tempeh, tofu)
Fibre	wholegrain flours, brown rice, quinoa, buckwheat, vegetables, fruits, avocado, legumes (beans, lentils, peas), nuts, seeds
Omega 3	seeds (chia, flax), leafy green vegetables, walnuts, omega eggs, organic milk
Calcium	low-oxalate leafy greens (broccoli, cabbage, kale, watercress), almonds, fortified plant milks, sesame seeds/tahini, figs, blackstrap molasses, dairy produce
Iron	legumes (beans, lentils, peas, peanuts), leafy greens, quinoa, potatoes, dried fruit, dark chocolate, tahini, seeds (pumpkin, sesame, sunflower), eggs, dairy produce
Zinc	legumes (beans, lentils, peas, peanuts), nuts (e.g. cashews, pecans, Brazil nuts, almonds), seeds, oats, eggs, dairy produce
Choline	legumes (beans, lentils, peas, peanuts), bananas, broccoli, oats, oranges, quinoa, eggs
Folate	leafy green vegetables, almonds, asparagus, avocado, beets, enriched grains (breads, pasta, rice), oranges, quinoa, nutritional yeast, eggs
Vitamin B12	nutritional yeast, plant milks, eggs, dairy produce
Vitamin C	fruits (especially berries, citrus, melon, kiwifruit, mango, papaya, pineapple), leafy green vegetables, potatoes, peas, (bell) peppers, chillies/chiles, tomatoes
Vitamin D	eggs, dairy produce, fortified foods
Vitamin K	leafy green vegetables, asparagus, avocado, broccoli, Brussels sprouts, cauliflower, lentils, peas

DAIRY ALTERNATIVES

Cashews bring a rich and creamy texture to these plant-based dairy cream alternatives. Both can be used in or alongside many of the dishes in this book; stirred into pasta, with a cake or on top of a smoky bean chilli, for example. The Vegan Cream recipe comes from my friend and inspiring recipe creator Jo at www.quirkycooking.com.

VEGAN SOUR CREAM

170 g/1¹/₂ cups cashews
   (soaked overnight
   in the fridge)
135 ml/9 tbsp water
1¹/₂ tsp apple cider
   vinegar
1¹/₂ tbsp lemon juice
¹/₄ tsp salt

Makes 4 servings

Combine all the ingredients in a food processor. You may need to do this in stages and keep bringing the mixture back into the centre of the processor. Process until you have a thick pouring cream consistency. Leave in the fridge to cool and thicken for 2 hours then use.

VEGAN CREAM

150 g/1¹/₄ cups cashews
   (unsoaked)
150 ml/10 tbsp water
1 tsp vanilla extract
1 tsp maple syrup

Makes 4 servings

Combine all the ingredients in a food processor until you have a pouring cream consistency. You can use this straight away, but it is best left to cool in the fridge for 2 hours before using.

PORRIDGES & DHALS

SPICED APPLE PORRIDGE Ⓥ

**100 g/1 cup porridge (rolled)/
old-fashioned oats**
**450 ml/scant 2 cups any milk of
your choice**
2 tbsp Apple Purée (see page 125)
1 eating apple, grated
1 tsp maple syrup
**1/2 tsp each ground cinnamon and
ground ginger**
1/8 tsp ground cloves
1 tsp chia seeds
**extra grated apple, maple syrup
and ground cinnamon, to serve
(optional)**

Serves 2–3

*A comforting Autumnal/Fall breakfast bowl, combining
oats, apples and warming spices.*

Place all the ingredients in a suitable heatproof bowl that
fits inside the Instant Pot inner pot and stir. Pour 250 ml/
1 cup water into the pot and pop the trivet on top. Place
the bowl of porridge ingredients on the trivet and set to
PRESSURE for 12 minutes. QPR at the end of cooking.

Serve with grated apple, maple syrup and a dusting
of cinnamon over the top, if liked.

SIMPLE POT-IN-POT PORRIDGE Ⓥ

**100 g/1 cup porridge (rolled)/
old-fashioned oats**
**450 ml/scant 2 cups any milk of
your choice**
pinch of salt
**coconut cream, Vegan Cream (see
page 11) or dairy cream, Apple
Purée (see page 125) and
ground flaxseeds, to serve
(optional)**

Serves 2–3

*A deliciously creamy porridge. Simply prepare the
ingredients then leave to cook while you get ready
for the day. Come back to find your porridge
perfectly cooked.*

Place the oats with the milk and salt in a suitable
heatproof bowl that fits inside the Instant Pot inner pot
and stir. Pour 500 ml/2 cups water into the pot and pop
the trivet on top. Place the bowl of porridge ingredients
on the trivet. Set to PRESSURE for 10 minutes. QPR at
the end of cooking.

Serve with coconut cream, Vegan Cream or dairy
cream, Apple Purée and a sprinkle of flaxseeds over the
top, if liked.

MANGO QUINOA
BREAKFAST BOWL ⓥ

170 g/1 cup quinoa flakes
1 x 400-g/14-oz. can coconut
   milk
200 g/7 oz. frozen mango chunks
1 tbsp maple syrup
1 tsp vanilla extract
100 g/³⁄₄ cup pistachio nuts
   (weight without shells and
   unsalted)
500 g/2 generous cups coconut
   yogurt or Greek yogurt
toasted coconut chips, to serve
   (optional)

Serves 8

This recipe is inspired by a 'grab and go' yogurt and quinoa breakfast that I have purchased at railway stations and service stations whilst travelling to or from workshops. It's a simple combination of delicious ingredients and brings with it the sweet mango and creamy yogurt with tropical tasting coconut.

Place all the ingredients (except the pistachio nuts and yogurt) straight into the Instant Pot inner pot. Set to PRESSURE for 2 minutes. Allow NPR at the end of cooking. Let the quinoa cool then stir in the nuts and yogurt.
   Serve with toasted coconut chips over the top, if liked.

CHOCO-NANA QUINOA
PORRIDGE ⓥ

1 banana, mashed
20 g/³⁄₄ oz. ground almonds
20 g/³⁄₄ oz. desiccated coconut
1 tbsp cocoa or cacao powder
100 ml/6 tablespoons any
   plant-based milk
20 g/³⁄₄ oz. quinoa flakes
¹⁄₄ tsp ground cinnamon
pinch of salt
cashew butter or Vegan Cream,
   (see page 11), to serve

Serves 1

This is a rich and chocolatey porridge for one that is extremely quick to make in the mornings. An express breakfast that is also a treat!

Place all the ingredients in a suitable heatproof bowl that fits inside the Instant Pot inner pot and stir. Pour 500 ml/ 2 cups water into the pot then pop the trivet on top. Place the bowl of porridge ingredients on the trivet. Set to PRESSURE for 3 minutes. QPR at the end of cooking.
   Serve with a drizzle of cashew butter or a dollop of Vegan Cream, as preferred.

CHAI & TURMERIC PORRIDGE ⓥ

100 g/1 cup porridge (rolled)/
   old-fashioned oats
250 ml/1 cup milk of your choice
250 ml/1 cup water
1/4 tsp each ground cinnamon,
   ground ginger, ground allspice
1/8 tsp turmeric
pinch of salt
1/2 tsp vanilla extract
1 banana, chopped
berries, sliced banana and honey
   or maple syrup, to serve
   (optional)

Serves 2–3

*This is a lightly spiced and aromatic porridge.
It makes a nice change from plain porridge and
brings you a reassuring, warming feeling.*

Place all the ingredients in a suitable heatproof bowl that
fits inside the Instant Pot inner pot and stir. Pour 500 ml/
2 cups water into the inner pot and pop in the trivet. Place
the bowl of porridge ingredients on top on the trivet. Set to
PRESSURE for 10 minutes and QPR at the end of cooking.

   Serve with berries, sliced banana and a drizzle of honey
or maple syrup over the top, if liked.

QUINOA & OAT SAVOURY PORRIDGE ⓥ

45 g/scant 1/2 cup porridge
   (rolled)/old-fashioned oats
45 g/scant 1/2 cup quinoa flakes
2 tbsp nutritional yeast flakes
1/4 tsp vegetable bouillon powder
8 cherry tomatoes, halved
390 ml/scant 1 3/4 cups milk of
   your choice
salt and ground black pepper,
   to season

Serves 2

*This is a delicious and wholesome savoury porridge.
It is made using little halves of cherry tomato and
nutritional yeast flakes which make for contrasting
sweet and tangy pops of flavour in an otherwise
smooth and creamy dish.*

Place all the ingredients (except the salt and pepper) into
a suitable heatproof bowl that fits inside the Instant Pot
inner pot and mix well. Pour 500 ml/2 cups water into the
pot and pop in the trivet. Place the bowl of porridge
ingredients on top of the trivet. Set to PRESSURE for 10
minutes and carry out a QPR at the end of cooking.

   Season to taste with salt and pepper and serve.

SAVOURY MUSHROOM & PEA PORRIDGE Ⓥ

100 g/1 cup porridge (rolled)/
   old-fashioned oats
450 ml/scant 2 cups any
   plant-based milk
1 tbsp olive oil
100 g/$^2/_3$ cup thinly sliced button
   mushrooms
1 tbsp frozen flat-leaf parsley
100 g/$^3/_4$ cup frozen peas
1 tbsp tamari or soy sauce
sliced avocado and extra soy or
   tamari sauce, to serve
   (optional)

Serves 2-3

Sautéed mushrooms and creamy oats make this savoury porridge a very satisfying meal.

Place the oats and milk in a suitable heatproof bowl that fits inside the Instant Pot inner pot, mix and set aside. Set the Instant Pot to SAUTÉ and heat the oil. Sauté the mushrooms for a few minutes then add the parsley and peas. Once the peas are defrosted remove the vegetables from the pot and stir them onto the bowl of oats.

Pour 500 ml/2 cups water into the pot and pop the trivet on top. Place the bowl of porridge ingredients on the trivet. Set to PRESSURE for 10 minutes. QPR at the end of cooking.

Serve with avocado slices and a drizzle of extra soy or tamari over the top, if liked.

SAVOURY LEEK PORRIDGE Ⓥ

100 g/1 cup porridge oats
400 ml/1$^3/_4$ cups any plant-based
   milk
2 tbsp nutritional yeast flakes
2 tbsp vegan spread or oil
1 large leek, thinly sliced
$^1/_8$ tsp salt
$^1/_4$ tsp lemon juice
extra sautéed leeks, Vegan Sour
   Cream (see recipe on page 11),
   to serve (optional)

Serves 2-3

See a photograph of this dish on page 11.

The cooked leeks and nutritional yeast flakes give this vegan porridge dish a decadent and comforting feel.

Place the oats, milk and yeast flakes in a suitable heatproof bowl that fits inside the Instant Pot inner pot, mix and set aside. Set the Instant Pot to SAUTÉ and heat the spread or oil. Add the leeks and salt and cook, stirring frequently, for about 5 minutes. When the leeks start to catch add the lemon juice, stir rapidly then remove from the pot and stir into the bowl of porridge ingredients.

Pour 500 ml/2 cups water into the pot and pop the trivet on top. Place the bowl of porridge ingredients on the trivet. Set to PRESSURE for 10 minutes. QPR at the end of cooking.

Serve topped with extra sautéed leeks and Vegan Sour Cream, if liked.

BUTTERNUT SQUASH & GREEN BEAN DHAL ⓥ

1 tsp nigella seeds
2 tsp olive oil
1 onion, chopped
1 green chilli/chile, chopped
2 tsp chopped garlic
1 tsp chopped fresh ginger
1 heaped tsp salt
1 tsp mild curry powder
1 tsp ground turmeric
1 butternut squash chopped into
    2-cm/³/₄-inch cubes
1 red (bell) pepper, chopped
8 cherry tomatoes, sliced in half
100 g/³/₄ cup frozen green beans
200 g/1 cup red lentils, rinsed
1 tsp vegetable bouillon powder
1 x 400-ml/14-oz. can coconut
    milk
375 ml/1¹/₂ cups water
yogurt or vegan yogurt, chopped
    coriander/cilantro and crispy
    fried shallots, to serve
    (optional)

Serves 4–6

A colourful and lightly spiced vegetable-packed dhal.

Set the Instant Pot to SAUTÉ. Add the nigella seeds to the pot and toast for 1 minute then add the oil, onion and chilli/chile. Stir for 3–4 minutes then add the garlic, ginger, salt, curry powder and turmeric. If the contents of the pot start to stick add a little of the coconut milk and deglaze.

Add the squash, (bell) pepper, cherry tomatoes and green beans and stir for a couple of minutes then add the lentils and bouillon powder, as well as the rest of the coconut milk and the water. Push the lentils under the liquid. Set to PRESSURE for 8 minutes and allow an NPR at the end of cooking.

Serve topped with yogurt, chopped coriander/cilantro and crispy fried shallots, if liked.

CREAMY MUNG BEAN DHAL ⓥ

100 g/¹/₂ cup dried mung beans,
    rinsed
1 tsp chopped fresh ginger
1 tsp chopped garlic
200 g/³/₄ cup passata (Italian
    strained tomatoes)
1 tsp salt
250 ml/1 cup water
3 tbsp coconut cream

Serves 4

A filling and wholesome bowl of food that is simplicity itself to make. Ideal served with some chapati bread or toasted wholegrain pitta.

Simply put all the ingredients (except the coconut cream) into the Instant Pot. Set to PRESSURE for 25 minutes.

Allow an NPR at the end of cooking then stir in the coconut cream and serve.

KITCHARI Ⓥ

190 g/1 cup brown rice
110 g/³⁄₄ cup chana dal
600 ml/2¹⁄₂ cups water
³⁄₄ tsp salt
1 tsp ground turmeric
1 tsp ground cumin
2 tbsp butter, vegan spread or oil
1 onion, chopped
2 tsp chopped garlic
1 tsp grated ginger
2 tsp chopped coriander/cilantro,
  plus extra, to serve

Serves 4

This is a simple, delicious and comforting dish combining chana dal (split chickpeas) and brown rice with some Indian spices and either butter or oil.

Place the rice, chana dal, water, salt, turmeric and cumin in the Instant Pot and set to PRESSURE for 20 minutes. NPR for 10 minutes at the end of cooking. Remove from the pot and set aside.

Heat the Instant Pot on SAUTÉ and add the butter, spread or oil followed by the onion and sauté for 3 minutes before adding the garlic, ginger and coriander/cilantro and sautéing for another few minutes. Make sure the onion is soft and transparent before stirring the rice and chana dal back into the pot.

Once the rice and chana dal are coated in the buttery/oily onions serve with the extra chopped coriander/cilantro scattered over the top.

SIMPLE RED LENTIL DHAL Ⓥ

2 tbsp olive oil
1 onion, finely chopped
2 tsp ground cumin
1 tsp salt
¹⁄₂ tsp ground turmeric
¹⁄₂ tsp ground coriander/cilantro
¹⁄₂ tsp garlic powder
215 g/1¹⁄₄ cups dried red lentils
600 ml/2¹⁄₂ cups water
yogurt or vegan yogurt and
  chopped coriander/cilantro,
  to serve (optional)

Serves 4

Dhal is one of the simplest pulse-based dishes to create as lentils cook so quickly and don't need to be pre-soaked. They provide a satisfying, creamy texture for those newer to plant-based eating too.

Heat the Instant Pot on SAUTÉ. Add the oil and sauté the onion for about 5 minutes, until soft. Press the CANCEL button then stir in the salt and spices followed by the lentils. Once the onions and lentils are well mixed with the spices and salt add the water and give everything a good stir. Add the lid and set to PRESSURE for 10 minutes. At the end of cooking leave to NPR for at least 10 minutes.

Serve topped with yogurt and chopped coriander/cilantro, if liked.

SOUPS & STEWS

SUMMER GREENS SOUP Ⓥ

2 tbsp olive oil
1 onion, chopped
600 ml/2¹/₂ cups water with
   1 vegetable stock cube
400 g/3 cups frozen peas
250 g/9 oz. Little Gem/Boston
   lettuce, roughly chopped
1 tbsp chopped mint, plus extra
   leaves to garnish
salt and pepper, to season
extra virgin olive oil, to serve
   (optional)

Serves 4

A light, fresh and vibrant soup for the summer months.

Set the Instant Pot to SAUTÉ. Add the oil then the onion and sauté for 3–5 minutes. Add all the other ingredients then set to PRESSURE for 1 minute. QPR at the end of cooking.

   Blend using a stick blender or food processor once cooled a little. Put back into the pot on SAUTÉ if you wish to reheat before serving.

   Season to taste with salt and pepper and serve with a drizzle of extra virgin olive oil and mint leaves to garnish, if liked.

CREAMY ASPARAGUS SOUP

2 tbsp butter
350 g/³/₄ lb. fresh asparagus,
   trimmed weight, cut into 4-cm/
   1¹/₂-inch pieces
1 onion, sliced
250 g/¹/₂ lb. new potatoes,
   unpeeled and cut into 2-cm/
   ³/₄-inch cubes
4 tsp vegetable bouillon powder
1 litre/4 cups water
1 tbsp lemon juice
100 ml/6 tbsp cream, plus extra
   to serve
ground black pepper, to season
finely shaved raw asparagus,
   to serve (optional)

Serves 4

See a photograph of this dish on page 6.

This is a deliciously seasonal spring dish. Just when asparagus is at its prime and new potatoes are a thing of distinct deliciousness combine the two in this creamy soup. It's a great way to use up those slightly thicker asparagus stalks. Keep the finer ones for dipping into soft boiled eggs (see page 100)!

Heat the Instant Pot on SAUTÉ and add the butter. Once melted add the asparagus, onion and potatoes. Sauté, stirring frequently for 5 minutes. Add the bouillon powder, water and lemon juice. Set to PRESSURE for 8 minutes then NPR for 5 minutes.

   Remove the lid, allow to cool a little then process in a food processor or with a stick blender. Stir in the cream then season to taste with pepper. Put back into the pot on SAUTÉ if you wish to reheat before serving.

   Serve with a swirl of cream and asparagus shavings (made using a vegetable peeler), if liked.

COURGETTE & PESTO SOUP

1 tbsp butter
1 onion, sliced
550 g/19 oz. courgettes/zucchini,
   thickly sliced
230 g/8 oz. white potatoes,
   peeled and cut into 1-cm/
   ½-inch cubes
1 vegetable stock cube
500 ml/2 cups water
1 x 145-g/5-oz. tub fresh
   vegetarian pesto
toasted pine nuts, to serve
   (optional)

Serves 4

A delightfully bright green bowl of goodness that tastes like summer in a soup.

Press the SAUTÉ button on the Instant Pot and melt the butter in the pot. Add the onion and sauté until it starts to brown slightly. Add all other ingredients (except the pesto). Set to PRESSURE for 4 minutes. Use NPR for 10 minutes at the end of cooking then release the remaining pressure.

Use a stick blender or food processor to blend the soup to a smooth consistency then stir in the pesto.

Serve with toasted pine nuts sprinkled over the top, if liked.

HARISSA, RED PEPPER & TOMATO SOUP ⓥ

1 tbsp oil
1 onion, chopped
2 red (bell) peppers, chopped
2 garlic cloves, peeled
850 g/1 lb. 14 oz. fresh tomatoes,
   quartered
1½ tbsp harissa paste
2 tsp vegetable bouillon powder
1 tsp maple syrup
¼ tsp apple cider vinegar
250 ml/1 cup water
vegan yogurt and chopped
   flat-leaf parsley, to serve

Serves 4-6

A delicious soup with a hint of the Middle East. The natural sweetness of the peppers and tomatoes is brought to bear alongside the spiciness of harissa paste.

Press SAUTÉ on the Instant Pot and add the oil then the onions, (bell) peppers and garlic. Sauté for about 5 minutes then add the tomatoes and cook, stirring occasionally, for about 5 minutes. Add the harissa paste, bouillon powder, maple syrup, apple cider vinegar and water and stir then set to PRESSURE for 10 minutes. QPR at the end of cooking.

Blend in a food processor or using a stick blender and serve with a swirl of vegan yogurt and chopped flat-leaf parsley, if liked.

FRESH TOMATO SOUP ⓥ

1 tbsp oil
3 celery sticks/stalks, chopped
2 carrots, chopped
1 onion, chopped
3 garlic cloves, peeled
850 g/1 lb. 14 oz. fresh tomatoes,
   quartered
2 tbsp nutritional yeast flakes
2 tbsp tomato purée/paste
1 tbsp balsamic vinegar
1 tsp maple syrup
1 vegetable stock cube
250 ml/1 cup water

Serves 4-6

This is a light soup made using lots and lots of fresh tomatoes. It is best enjoyed in the spring and summer months when the tomatoes are at their ripest for the best and fullest flavour. The nutritional yeast makes this soup taste creamy. It is almost like a very famous brand of cream of tomato soup!

Press SAUTÉ on the Instant Pot and add the oil then the celery, carrots, onions and garlic. Sauté for about 5 minutes then add the tomatoes and cook, stirring occasionally, for about 5 minutes. Add the nutritional yeast flakes, tomato purée/paste, balsamic vinegar, maple syrup, vegetable stock cube and water and stir then set to PRESSURE for 10 minutes. QPR at the end of cooking.

Blend in a food processor or using a stick blender once cooled a little. Put back into the pot on SAUTÉ if you wish to reheat before serving.

SWEETCORN CHOWDER ⓥ

1 tbsp olive oil
1 onion, roughly chopped
1 orange (bell) pepper, chopped
1 celery stick/stalk, chopped
1/2–1 tsp chilli/chile paste
300 g/2 cups frozen sweetcorn/
   corn
2 tsp frozen coriander/cilantro
600 ml/2 1/2 cups water
1 vegetable stock cube
1 tsp smoked paprika
160 ml/2/3 cup coconut cream
smoked paprika and snipped
   chives, to serve (optional)

Serves 4

Sweet but with a little bit of heat! This smoky flavoured chowder is quick and easy and ever so satisfying.

Set the Instant Pot to SAUTÉ. Heat the oil and add the onion then sauté for 3–5 minutes, stirring occasionally. Add all the other ingredients except the coconut cream. Set to PRESSURE for 2 minutes. QPR at the end of cooking.

Blend using a stick blender or food processor once cooled a little, then stir in the coconut cream. Put back into the pot on SAUTÉ if you wish to reheat before serving.

Serve with a dusting of smoked paprika and a sprinkle of snipped chives, if liked.

FENNEL & CARROT SOUP ⓥ

1 tbsp garlic-infused olive oil
1 fennel bulb, sliced thinly (fronds
   reserved to serve)
1 onion, roughly chopped
1 tsp chopped fresh ginger
3 carrots, chopped
600 ml/2 1/2 cups water
1 vegetable stock cube
ground black pepper, to season

Serves 4

See a photograph of this dish on page 5.

This soup provides a great flavour combination from the mild aniseed taste of the fennel to the sweet taste of the carrots and a little spicy heat from the ginger.

Set the Instant Pot to SAUTÉ. Heat the oil add the fennel and onion and sauté for 2–3 minutes. Add all the other ingredients and set the pot to PRESSURE for 6 minutes with QPR at the end of cooking.

Use a stick blender or food processor to process the soup once cooled a little. Put back into the pot on SAUTÉ if you wish to reheat before serving.

Serve with a good twist of black pepper and the reserved fennel fronds over the top.

PULLED BBQ JACKFRUIT WITH PINTO BEANS Ⓥ

1 tbsp garlic-infused olive oil
1 onion, chopped
4 carrots, chopped
2 celery sticks/stalks, chopped
100 g/¹/₃ cup frozen sweetcorn/
    corn
2 x 400-g/14-oz. cans jackfruit,
    drained and shredded
1 x 400-g/14-oz. can pinto beans,
    drained and rinsed
1 tbsp soy sauce
3 tbsp any BBQ sauce
250 g/1 cup passata (Italian
    strained tomatoes)
brown rice, Vegan Sour Cream
    (see page 11) and snipped
    chives, to serve (optional)

Serves 2

Jackfruit has a texture which is rather like pulled pork. It lends itself to similar flavours being used with it in dishes as you might expect its meaty counterpart to be included. However, it is, as the name suggests, a fruit. It makes for a delicious plant-based dish with a rich flavour and texture.

Set the Instant Pot to SAUTÉ. Heat the oil and sauté the onion, carrots and celery for 5 minutes. Add all of the remaining ingredients and set the pot to PRESSURE for 6 minutes. NPR at the end of cooking.

    Serve with brown rice, a dollop of Vegan Sour Cream and snipped chives, if liked.

VEGAN SAUSAGE & POTATO STEW Ⓥ

1 tbsp vegan spread or olive oil
1 onion, cut into wedges
6 plant-based sausages
250 g/9 oz. carrots, cut into
    thick slices
250 g/9 oz. potatoes, unpeeled
    and cut into 3-cm/1¹/₄-inch
    cubes
300 ml/1¹/₄ cups water
1 tsp vegetable bouillon powder
³/₄ tsp dried thyme

Serves 2

Sausage and potato stew is the taste of my childhood. This version uses vegan sausages and is immensely comforting and filling.

Set the Instant Pot to SAUTÉ. Heat the oil then add the onion and sausages. Sauté until the sausages start to stick a little to the bottom of the pot then add the carrots, potatoes, water, bouillon powder and thyme. Set the pot to PRESSURE for 10 minutes. QPR at the end of cooking.

    Serve straightaway.

MIDDLE EASTERN FAVA BEAN STEW ⓥ

1 tbsp oil
1 onion, roughly chopped
2 garlic cloves, chopped
250 g/9 oz. butternut squash,
    cut into 1-cm/½-inch cubes
1 tbsp rose harissa paste
1 tbsp maple syrup
1 x 400-g/14-oz. can chopped
    tomatoes
1 x 400-g/14-oz can broad/fava
    beans, drained and rinsed
1 tsp salt
1 bay leaf
¼ tsp dried chilli/hot pepper flakes
75 ml/5 tbsp water
vegan yogurt and toasted pitta
    bread, to serve (optional)

Serves 4

Wonderfully aromatic rose harissa combines with sweet and satisfying butternut squash, maple syrup and tomatoes to really bring out the beautiful flavours and textures in this Middle Eastern dish.

Set the Instant Pot to SAUTÉ. Heat the oil add the onion, garlic and squash, and sauté for 5 minutes. Add all the remaining ingredients and set the pot to PRESSURE for 5 minutes. NPR at the end of cooking.

   Serve with a swirl of vegan yogurt and toasted pitta bread, if liked.

MOROCCAN LENTIL STEW ⓥ

1 tbsp olive oil
1 onion, chopped
100 g/3½ oz. mushrooms,
    chopped
1 courgette/zucchini, chopped
6 plum tomatoes, chopped
1 tbsp rose harissa paste
2 tbsp tomato purée/paste
1 tbsp honey
pinch of saffron threads
1 tsp smoked paprika
1 tsp ground cumin
½ tsp ground coriander/cilantro
1 tsp salt
1 x 250-g/9-oz. pouch simply
    cooked Puy lentils
50 ml/3½ tbsp water
1 x 250-g/9-oz. bag baby spinach
chopped flat-leaf parsley,
    to serve (optional)

Serves 2

An aromatic and smoky flavoured stew made with satisfying Puy lentils and North African spicing.

Heat the Instant Pot on SAUTÉ then add the olive oil and sauté the onion and mushrooms until they start to release their liquid. Add the courgettes/zucchini and tomatoes and sauté for another 3–5 minutes allowing the tomatoes to break down a little.

   Add the harissa paste, tomato purée/paste, honey, saffron, paprika, cumin, coriander, salt, Puy lentils and the water. Set to PRESSURE for 2 minutes. QPR at the end of cooking, then stir in the baby spinach until wilted.

   To serve, scatter chopped flat-leaf parsley over the top, if liked.

CHICKPEA, POTATO & TOMATO SAFFRON STEW Ⓥ

1 tbsp olive oil

1 onion

2 garlic cloves, thinly sliced

1 tbsp tomato purée/paste

pinch of saffron threads

200-g/7 oz. potatoes cut into 1-cm/½-inch cubes

400-g/14-oz. can chickpeas, drained and rinsed

400-g/14-oz. can chopped tomatoes

1 heaped tsp vegetable bouillon powder

chopped flat-leaf parsley and lemon wedges, to serve (optional)

Serves 3–4

Tomatoes and saffron bring a Mediterranean feel to this satisfying chickpea stew.

Set the Instant Pot to SAUTÉ and add the oil then sauté the onions and garlic. Stir well until the onions are almost transparent then add the tomato purée/paste, saffron, potatoes, chickpeas, tomatoes and bouillon powder. Set to PRESSURE for 4 minutes. NPR at the end of cooking.

To serve, scatter chopped flat-leaf parsley over the top and add lemon wedges for squeezing, if liked.

MEDITERRANEAN LENTIL STEW Ⓥ

1 tbsp olive oil

2 celery sticks/stalks, chopped

2 carrots, finely chopped

250 g/9 oz. mushrooms, sliced

2 tbsp tomato purée/paste

2 tbsp nutritional yeast flakes

1 tbsp balsamic vinegar

1 tbsp maple syrup

1 tsp salt

1 tsp dried chilli/hot pepper flakes

pinch of saffron threads

½ tsp garlic powder

250 g/1½ cups split red lentils

350 g/1½ cups passata (Italian strained tomatoes)

500 ml/2 cups water

brown rice, to serve (optional)

Serves 4

An easy recipe yet a wholesome and satisfying stew full of the sunshine flavours of the Mediterranean.

Set the Instant Pot to SAUTÉ and add the oil then once hot sauté the celery and carrots for 5 minutes. Add the mushrooms and sauté, stirring regularly, until they start to release their liquid.

Add all the remaining ingredients then set to PRESSURE for 4 minutes. Use NPR at the end of cooking.

Serve with brown rice, if liked.

CURRIES & CHILLIES

CAULIFLOWER MASALA Ⓥ

1 tbsp vegan spread or oil
1 onion, chopped
1 tsp garam masala
½ tsp each ground turmeric and ground cumin
2 tsp chopped fresh ginger
1 tsp chopped garlic
2 tsp chopped coriander/cilantro, plus extra to serve
½ tsp salt
100 g/scant ½ cup passata (Italian strained tomatoes)
1 cauliflower, broken into florets
1 tsp maple syrup
100 ml/6 tbsp water
sliced red onion, coconut yogurt, flaked/slivered almonds and poppadoms, to serve (optional)

Serves 2

Cauliflower is synonymous with Indian cooking and this cauliflower curry is a delicious combination of aromatic Indian spices and a sweet, tangy sauce.

Set the Instant Pot to SAUTÉ and add the oil or spread to the pot. Add the onion and sauté for 3–5 minutes. Add the spices, ginger, garlic, coriander/cilantro and salt, and stir well then add the passata and stir again. Add the cauliflower, maple syrup and water then give everything a final stir. Set the pot to PRESSURE for 2 minutes with a QPR at the end of cooking.

Serve with all or any of the suggested garnishes and/or accompaniments, as preferred.

CAULIFLOWER & POTATO CURRY Ⓥ

1 tbsp olive oil
1 onion, chopped
1 garlic clove, chopped
1 tsp chopped fresh ginger
400 g/14 oz. potatoes, peeled and chopped into 1.5-cm/ ¾-inch cubes
1 cauliflower, broken into large florets
1 tsp cumin seeds
1 tsp ground coriander
½ tsp ground cumin
1 tsp ground turmeric
½ tsp cayenne pepper
1 green chilli/chile, finely chopped
3 plum tomatoes, chopped
1 tbsp tomato purée/paste
1 tsp salt
100 ml/6 tbsp water
salt and ground black pepper, to season

Serves 4

A classic combination of cauliflower and potato provides great texture to this simple plant-based curry.

Set the Instant Pot to SAUTÉ. Add the oil then sauté the onion for 3–5 minutes. Add the garlic and ginger then after 1 minute add the potatoes, cauliflower, spices, chilli/chile, tomatoes, tomato purée/paste, salt and water. Set to PRESSURE for 3 minutes and carry out a QPR at the end of cooking.

Season to taste and serve.

CARROT & GREEN BEAN CURRY Ⓥ

1 tbsp oil
1 onion, sliced
150 g/5½ oz. green beans, each
    1 cut into 3 pieces
2 large carrots, cut into 1-cm/
    ½-inch cubes
1 tsp grated fresh ginger
2 tsp chopped garlic
2 tbsp tomato purée/paste
1½ tsp chilli/chili paste
1 tsp salt
80 ml/5½ tbsp water
160 ml/⅔ cup coconut cream
'Buttery' Brown Basmati (see
    page 121) and simple vegan
    yogurt, cucumber and mint
    raita, to serve (optional)

Serves 4

This is a simple vegan curry celebrating the start of summer, made with green beans and carrots.

Set the Instant Pot to SAUTÉ and add the oil then the onion, green beans and carrots. Sauté for 5 minutes then add the ginger and garlic, and stir for 1 minute before adding the tomato purée/paste, chilli/chili paste, salt and water. Stir then set to PRESSURE for 3 minutes. QPR at the end of cooking and stir in the coconut cream. (If you want the curry sauce a little thicker set the pot to SAUTÉ until it has thickened a little.)

Serve with 'Buttery' Brown Basmati and cucumber and mint raita, if liked.

QUICK MILD VEGETABLE CURRY Ⓥ

100 g/3½ oz. green beans, each
    1 cut into 3 pieces
1 cauliflower, chopped into
    medium florets
1 onion, finely chopped
1 tbsp chopped fresh ginger
1 tbsp chopped garlic
1 tbsp chopped coriander/cilantro
10 cherry tomatoes, halved
1 carrot, chopped
2 potatoes, peeled and chopped
1 tsp salt
2 tsp curry powder
80 ml/5½ tbsp water
160 ml/⅔ cup coconut cream
Vegetable Pilaff (see page 121),
    to serve (optional)

Serves 4

This is a 'Dump and Go' recipe. That simply means you put everything into the pot and press a button then walk away. These are great recipes for extremely busy people, and this is a go-to recipe for my own family when we have lots of vegetables to use up but extraordinarily little time to cook.

Put all the ingredients (except the coconut cream) into the Instant Pot and set to PRESSURE for 3 minutes. QPR at the end of cooking and open the lid then stir in the coconut cream.

Serve with Vegetable Pilaff, if liked.

1 tbsp oil

2 x 225-g/8-oz. packs halloumi
  cheese, cut into 2-cm/³/₄-inch
  cubes

1 onion, roughly chopped

3 medium tomatoes, chopped

300 g/10¹/₂ oz. frozen spinach
  in blocks (frozen weight)

1 tsp chopped fresh ginger

2 tsp chopped garlic

2 tbsp tomato purée/paste

50 ml/3¹/₂ tbsp water

2 tbsp mild curry paste

¹/₄ tsp salt

1 x 400-g/14 oz. can chickpeas,
  drained and rinsed

toasted flaked/slivered almonds
  and lemon wedges, to serve
  (optional)

Serves 4

HALLOUMI, CHICKPEA & SPINACH CURRY

Whilst paneer is a more traditional Indian cheese used in curries, we enjoy Cypriot halloumi in curries too. In this dish it brings great texture and a little welcome saltiness too.

Heat the oil on the Instant Pot SAUTÉ setting. Add the cubed halloumi. Expect it to release a lot of water then after about 5 minutes of intermittent stirring watch over it as it starts to brown. Remove from the pot in the next couple of minutes once the pieces have browned a little and set aside.

Add the onions and tomatoes to the pot and deglaze using the juices from the tomatoes. Add the spinach, ginger, garlic, tomato paste/purée, water, curry paste, salt and chickpeas. Give everything a good stir then set to PRESSURE for 2 minutes. QPR at the end of cooking and stir the browned halloumi back into the curry.

Serve with toasted almonds scattered over the top and lemon wedges for squeezing, if liked.

1 tbsp oil

1 onion, chopped

¹/₂ vegetable stock cube

180 ml/³/₄ cup water

2 sweet potatoes, cut into
  2-cm/³/₄-inch cubes

1–2 tbsp vegan massaman
  curry paste

250-g/9-oz. block firm tofu,
  pressed and cut into cubes
  (see Note)

100 ml/6 tbsp coconut cream

100 g/1 cup frozen peas,
  defrosted

chopped Thai basil and flaked/
  slivered almonds, to serve
  (optional)

Serves 4

TOFU MASSAMAN Ⓥ

An aromatic and creamy Thai curry for vegans.

Heat the oil on the Instant Pot SAUTÉ setting. Once the oil is hot add the onion and sauté for about 5 minutes. Then crumble in the half stock cube and add the water, potatoes and curry paste. Set to 2 minutes at PRESSURE. QPR at the end of cooking. Stir in the tofu, coconut cream and peas.

Serve with chopped Thai basil and almonds scattered over the top, if liked.

NOTE: If you like a firmer texture on your tofu you can pan fry it in a non-stick frying pan/skillet in 1 tbsp oil, turning regularly until browned – this should take about 10 minutes. If you try and sauté the tofu in the Instant Pot it will stick to the bottom so it must be done separately.

VEGETABLE KORMA Ⓥ

1 tbsp oil
1 onion, chopped
200 g/7 oz. mushrooms, chopped
2 tomatoes, chopped
100 g/3½ oz. green beans,
   trimmed
2 tsp chopped fresh ginger
2 tbsp korma curry paste
120 ml/scant ½ cup water
2 medium sweet potatoes,
   chopped into 2-cm/¾-inch
   cubes
160 ml/⅔ cup coconut cream
Gram Flour Pancakes, to serve
   (see recipe below)

Serves 4

Quick, easy and economical to make. This creamy and mildly spiced vegetable curry is a simple dish that is made in minutes.

Heat the Instant Pot on SAUTÉ and add the oil to the pot. Add the onion and mushrooms and stir well. Cook for 4 minutes, stirring well then add the tomatoes and stir once more. Once the tomatoes start to break down add the green beans, ginger, curry paste, water and sweet potatoes. Give everything a good stir then set the pot to PRESSURE for 3 minutes. Carry out a QPR at the end of cooking then stir in the coconut cream.
   Serve with Gram Flour Pancakes (see below), if liked.

GRAM FLOUR PANCAKES Ⓥ

230 g/heaped 1¾ cups gram/
   chickpea flour
1 tsp baking powder
1 tsp salt
400 ml/1¾ cups water
1 tsp oil, for frying

Serves 4 (makes 8 pancakes)

Here is a bonus non-Instant Pot recipe for you to try as these gluten-free pancakes are easy to make and go particularly well with all the curries in this book.

Mix all the ingredients together well. Heat the oil in a frying pan/skillet. Pour sufficient batter into the hot pan to form a disc about 10 cm/4 inches in diameter. Once bubbles appear on the surface turn the pancake over and cook on the other side for a few more minutes. Continue until you have cooked all the batter.

NOTE: This recipe makes 8 pancakes so allow 2 per serving of any curry.

GREEN THAI TOFU CURRY ⓥ

1 tbsp oil
60 g/2 oz. shallots, finely chopped
2 tsp chopped garlic
1 tsp grated fresh ginger
2 celery sticks/stalks, chopped
40 g/2 tbsp green curry paste
250 g/ butternut squash, cut
   into 1-cm/¹/₂-inch cubes
1 tbsp soy sauce
125 ml/¹/₂ cup water
250-g/9-oz. block firm tofu,
   pressed and cut into cubes
   (see Note on page 49)
handful of beansprouts (optional)
1 tsp coconut or brown sugar
180 ml/³/₄ cup coconut milk
'Buttery' Brown Basmati (see
   page 121), Thai basil sprigs and
   lime wedges, to serve (optional)

Serves 4

An aromatic Thai curry with the addition of satisfying and filling tofu.

Set the Instant Pot to SAUTÉ and add the oil. When the oil is hot add the shallots, garlic, ginger and celery, and sauté for 3 minutes. Press CANCEL then add the curry paste, squash, soy sauce and water, and set to PRESSURE for 3 minutes with a QPR at the end of cooking. Set to SAUTÉ once more and stir in the tofu, beansprouts (if using), sugar and coconut milk. Stir until heated through.

Top with Thai Basil sprigs and serve with 'Buttery' Brown Basmati on the side and lime wedges for squeezing, if liked.

RED THAI VEGETABLE CURRY ⓥ

1 tbsp olive oil
1 onion, chopped
1 celery stick/stalk, chopped
1 tbsp vegan Thai red curry paste
1 tbsp soy sauce
1 tsp coconut sugar
¹/₂ tsp ginger purée/paste
400-g/14 oz. sweet potatoes,
   cut in 2-cm/³/₄-inch cubes
100 g/3¹/₂ oz. green beans, each
   1 cut into 3 pieces
50 ml/3¹/₂ tbsp water
1 tbsp peanut butter
100 ml/6 tbsp coconut milk
100 g/1 cup frozen peas, defrosted
chopped coriander/cilantro and
   brown rice or quinoa, to serve
   (optional)

Serves 2

A great mid-week meal with few steps and short cooking time.

Heat the Instant Pot on SAUTÉ. Add the oil to the pot then the onion and celery. Stir for about 5 minutes until the onions are becoming translucent. Meanwhile stir the curry paste, soy sauce, sugar and ginger together in a small bowl and add this next. Stir then add the sweet potatoes and green beans plus the water and stir again. Secure the lid in place and set to PRESSURE for 2 minutes. QPR at the end of cooking and stir in the peanut butter. Once it has melted a little add the coconut milk and peas.

Serve topped with chopped coriander/cilantro and with brown rice or quinoa on the side, if liked.

1 tbsp oil
1 onion, chopped
1 tsp chopped garlic
1 tsp chopped fresh ginger
2 tbsp tomato purée/paste
2 tbsp vegan tikka curry paste
2 sweet potatoes, cut into
    2-cm/¾-inch cubes
1 x 400-g/14-oz. can chickpeas
¾ tsp salt
100 ml/6 tbsp water
2 heaped tbsp peanut butter,
    softened
100 ml/6 tbsp coconut cream
2 tbsp chopped coriander/
    cilantro, plus extra to garnish
mini poppadoms, to serve
    (optional)

Serves 2

SWEET POTATO & CHICKPEA SATAY CURRY ⓥ

This is a deliciously rich curry with a blend of peanut butter, coconut cream and tikka spices brought together with wholesome chickpeas and starchy sweet potato.

Heat the Instant Pot on SAUTÉ and add the oil then the onion and sauté for 3–5 minutes. Add the garlic and ginger then the tomato purée/paste and curry paste. Stir then add the sweet potatoes, chickpeas, salt and water then set the pot to PRESSURE for 2 minutes. QPR at the end of cooking then stir in the peanut butter, coconut cream and coriander/cilantro.

Serve with chopped coriander/cilantro scattered over the top and mini poppadoms on the side, if liked.

1 tbsp oil
2 shallots, finely chopped
2 tsp chopped garlic
1 tsp each grated fresh turmeric
    and grated fresh ginger
2 celery sticks/stalks, chopped
1 tsp garam masala
½ tsp ground coriander/cilantro
1½ tsp coconut sugar
1 tsp salt
250 g/9 oz. butternut squash,
    cut into 2-cm/¾-inch cubes
190 g/1 cup split red lentils
600 ml/2½ cups water
2 heaped tbsp peanut butter
red chillies/chiles, spring onions/
    scallions and brown rice, to
    serve (optional)

Serves 4

INDONESIAN LENTIL CURRY ⓥ

A rich and nutty Indonesian curry. The textures of the lentils, vegetables and peanut butter create a rich bowl of deliciousness.

Set the Instant Pot to SAUTÉ and heat the oil then add the shallots, garlic, turmeric, ginger and celery, and sauté for 2 minutes then press CANCEL. Add the spices, sugar, salt, squash, lentils and water and stir then set the pot to PRESSURE for 8 minutes. QPR then stir in the peanut butter. Top topped with finely sliced red chillies/chiles and spring onions/scallions and serve with brown rice, if liked.

See a photograph of this dish on page 3.

2 tbsp olive oil
1 onion, chopped
1 aubergine/eggplant, cut into
    3-cm/1¹/₄-inch cubes
¹/₂–1 green chilli/chile, chopped
1 tsp chopped garlic
1 tsp chopped fresh ginger
1 large potato, cut into cubes
10 cherry tomatoes, quartered
1 tbsp tomato purée/paste
1 tsp mild curry powder
¹/₂ tsp each ground cumin, ground
    turmeric and garam masala
1 tsp salt
80 ml/5¹/₂ tbsp water
'Buttery' Brown Basmati (see
    page 121), lime pickle, sliced
    green chillies/chiles and
    coriander/cilantro leaves,
    to serve (optional)

Serves 4

AUBERGINE, TOMATO & POTATO CURRY ⓥ

A combination of comforting textures and aromatic spices. Aubergine/eggplant provides a buttery and succulent texture to contrast with the sweet cooked tomatoes and satisfying potatoes.

Set the Instant Pot to SAUTÉ and add the oil. Add the onion and sauté for 3–5 minutes stirring from time to time. Add the aubergine/eggplant, chilli/chile, garlic and ginger, and stir again. Do so until the aubergine/eggplant appears to have absorbed the oil. Add the cubed potato, cherry tomatoes, tomato purée/ paste and spices with the salt and stir again. You may need to add the water straightaway if the ingredients have started to stick. Stir in the water and set to PRESSURE for 4 minutes. NPR at the end of cooking for at least 15 minutes.

Serve with all or any of the suggested garnishes and/or accompaniments, as preferred.

1 tbsp olive oil or coconut oil
1 red onion, chopped
1 tbsp chopped garlic
2 tsp grated fresh ginger
1 tbsp frozen coriander/cilantro
3 fresh plum tomatoes, chopped
1 tbsp tomato purée/paste
1 tsp mild curry paste
¹/₂ tsp each garam masala,
    ground cumin, smoked paprika
¹/₄ tsp ground turmeric
1 heaped tsp salt
1 x 250-g/9-oz. potato, unpeeled
    and roughly chopped
1 x 400-g/14-oz can chickpeas,
    drained and rinsed
170 ml/scant ³/₄ cup water
85 ml/5¹/₂ tbsp coconut cream

Serves 4

CHICKPEA & POTATO CURRY ⓥ

This recipe is ideal for those cold and wet winter nights when you want a warm and comforting curry to keep you insulated.

Set the Instant Pot to SAUTÉ and add the oil. Add the onion and sauté for 5 minutes. Add the garlic, ginger and coriander/ cilantro. Stir and cook for 1 minute. Add the tomatoes, tomato purée/paste, curry paste, spices and salt and stir. Leave with the lid on for a further 3 minutes. Add the potato, chickpeas and water. Stir and cook on PRESSURE for 6 minutes. Leave to NPR at the end.

Stir in the coconut cream and serve.

SMOKY PINTO BEAN CHILLI ⓥ

1 tbsp oil

1 onion, chopped

250-g/9 oz. butternut squash, cut into 5-mm/¼-inch cubes

2 celery sticks/stalks, finely chopped

1 tsp each ground cumin and smoked paprika

¼ tsp ground cinnamon

½ tsp garlic powder

1 tsp salt

1 tbsp nutritional yeast flakes

1 heaped tsp raw cacao powder

1 tbsp blackstrap molasses

2 tbsp tomato purée/paste

1 tsp chilli/chili paste

1 x 400-g/14-oz. can pinto beans, drained and rinsed

200 g/¾ cup passata (Italian strained tomatoes)

170 ml/scant ¾ cup water

Vegan Sour Cream (see page 11), guacamole and sliced fresh green chillies/chiles, to serve (optional)

Serves 4

This rich, sweet and smoky pinto bean chilli/chili combines a touch of chilli with pleasing chocolatey and 'cheesy' vegan flavours.

Heat the oil in the Instant Pot on SAUTÉ. Sauté the onion, squash and celery for 5 minutes. Add the spices, garlic powder, salt, nutritional yeast flakes, cacao powder, molasses, tomato purée/paste, chilli/chili paste, pinto beans and passata plus the water. Set to PRESSURE for 7 minutes. NPR at the end of cooking.

Serve with all or any of the suggested garnishes and/or accompaniments, as preferred.

1 tbsp olive oil
1 onion, diced
375 g/13 oz. butternut squash,
    cut into 5-mm/¼-inch cubes
2 courgettes/zucchini, diced
2 tbsp tomato purée/paste
1 garlic clove, finely chopped
1 tsp each ground cumin and
    smoked paprika
¼ tsp ground cinnamon
1 tsp chilli/chili paste
1 tsp honey or maple syrup
1 x 400-g/14-oz. can chopped
    tomatoes
2 x 400-g/14-oz. cans black
    beans, drained and rinsed
1 vegetable stock cube
150 ml/⅔ cup water
Vegan Sour Cream (see page 11)
    grated vegan cheese, avocado
    slices, tortilla chips, chopped
    coriander/cilantro, lime
    wedges, to serve (optional)

Serves 4

BLACK BEAN CHILLI WITH BUTTERNUT SQUASH Ⓥ

Warming and filling. Texture-full black beans and sweet butternut squash are combine in this flavoursome meal.

Heat the oil in the Instant Pot on SAUTÉ. Add the onion, squash and courgettes/zucchini and sauté for 5 minutes. Add all the remaining ingredients and stir.

Close the lid. Cook on PRESSURE for 4 minutes, NPR at the end of cooking.

Serve with all or any of the suggested garnishes and/or accompaniments, as preferred.

1 tbsp olive oil
1 red onion, chopped
2 celery sticks/stalks, chopped
2 carrots, chopped
1 yellow (bell) pepper, chopped
½ tsp each garlic powder, chilli/
    chili powder, ground cumin
    and dried oregano
1 tsp smoked paprika
1 x 400-g/14-oz. can chopped
    tomatoes
250 g/1¼ cups brown rice, rinsed
150 g/1 cup dried black beans
1½ vegetable stock cubes
750 ml/3 cups water

Serves 6

BLACK BEANS & RICE Ⓥ

This is comfort in a bowl. The beans and rice cook together in a warming and protein-rich dish.

Set the Instant Pot to SAUTÉ and add the oil. Once hot add the onion, celery, carrots and (bell) pepper. Sauté for about 5 minutes. Stir in the garlic powder, chilli/chili powder, cumin, oregano and paprika. Add the tomatoes, rice and beans. Crumble in the vegetable stock cubes and add the water. Set the pot to PRESSURE for 30 minutes. Allow NPR for 10 minutes at the end.

Serve with all or any of the suggested garnishes and/or accompaniments for the recipe above, as preferred.

MEXICAN BLACK BEAN & CHOCOLATE CHILLI Ⓥ

2 tbsp oil
1 onion, chopped
1 red (bell) pepper, chopped
1 aubergine/eggplant, chopped
½ tsp each ground cumin and ground coriander
1 tsp chopped garlic
1 x 400-g/14-oz. can black beans, drained and rinsed
1 x 400-g/14-oz. can chopped tomatoes
1 tbsp soy sauce
30 g/2 tbsp grated vegan dark chocolate
brown rice, Vegan Sour Cream (see page 11), finely sliced red onion, diced avocado, coriander/cilantro and tortilla chips, to serve (optional)

Serves 4

A delicious and comforting dish made with black beans that give a wholesome texture to this meal and a little dark chocolate for depth of flavour.

Set the Instant Pot to SAUTÉ and add the oil then the onion, (bell) pepper and aubergine/eggplant. If the ingredients start to stick a little (aubergine/eggplant tends to act like a sponge to oil and suck it all up) then adjust the sauté to LOWER using the SAUTÉ button or dial. Sauté until the aubergine/eggplant is soft and the onion transparent. Add the spices and garlic then the beans, tomatoes and soy sauce. Set to PRESSURE for 3 minutes. NPR at the end of cooking then remove the lid and stir in the chocolate.

Serve with all or any of the suggested garnishes and/or accompaniments, as preferred.

RICE & QUINOA

VEGAN MUSHROOM RISOTTO ⓥ

1 tbsp oil
1 onion, chopped
250 g/9 oz. mushrooms, sliced
1 tbsp chopped garlic
250 g/1¼ cups Arborio rice
75 ml/scant ⅓ cup vegan
　white wine
550 ml/scant 2¼ cups water
1 tsp vegetable bouillon powder
3 tbsp nutritional yeast flakes
1 tbsp chopped flat-leaf parsley,
　plus extra to serve
a salad, to serve (optional)

Serves 4

Although risotto is probably most associated with a rich and creamy texture brought about by the addition of butter and cheese, a deliciously rich and 'cheesy' risotto can also be created with sautéed mushrooms and the addition of nutritional yeast flakes, making this a dish suitable for vegans.

Set the Instant Pot to SAUTÉ and add the oil to the pot. Add the onion and sauté for 3 minutes before adding the mushrooms and garlic. Keep sautéing until the mushrooms release their liquid and then add the rice and stir. As soon as the rice is combined with the other ingredients add the wine and stir. The wine will evaporate and once it has pour in the water, vegetable bouillon and yeast flakes and stir once again. Set the pot to PRESSURE for 6 minutes. QPR at the end of cooking and stir in the chopped parsley.

　Serve garnished with extra chopped flat-leaf parsley over the top and with a salad on the side, if liked.

LEEK & MUSHROOM RISOTTO

50 g/3½ tbsp salted butter, plus
    extra to serve
3 slim leeks, rinsed and sliced
250 g/1¼ cups Arborio rice
75 ml/scant ⅓ cup white wine
1 vegetable stock cube
550 ml/scant 2¼ cups water
1 tbsp chopped flat-leaf parsley
250-g/9 oz. mushrooms, thickly
    sliced
1 x 250-g/9-oz. pack baby
    spinach
70 g/2½ oz. vegetarian Parmesan
    cheese, finely grated plus extra
    to serve
a salad, to serve (optional)

Serves 4

There are few foods in life more comforting than buttery leeks. They simply melt in the mouth in this simple leek and mushroom risotto.

Set the Instant Pot to SAUTÉ and add the butter to the pot. Once melted add the leeks and sauté until soft and browning. Add the rice and stir well then add the wine and stock cube. Stir again then add the water, chopped parsley and mushrooms. Secure the lid in place then set to PRESSURE for 6 minutes. Use QPR at the end of cooking. Stir in the spinach, cheese and extra butter to taste.

Serve sprinkled with extra grated cheese and a salad on the side, if liked.

GARLIC, SPINACH & MUSHROOM BROWN RICE Ⓥ

190 g/1 cup brown rice, rinsed
250 ml/1 cup water
1 tbsp vegan spread or butter
1 tbsp oil
250 g/9 oz. button mushrooms,
    sliced
120 g/2 cups chopped fresh
    spinach
2 garlic cloves, chopped
½ tsp salt

Serves 4

A straight-forward, deliciously satisfying and wholesome rice dish that can be enjoyed as a side with many of the recipes in this book.

Put the rice and water in the Instant Pot inner pot and set to PRESSURE for 15 minutes. NPR for 15 minutes or until the valve drops whichever is first. Remove the rice and set aside.

Press SAUTÉ on the pot then add the vegan spread or butter, oil, mushrooms, spinach, garlic and salt. As soon as the mushrooms release their liquid put the rice back into the pot and stir well before serving.

GREEN HERB RISOTTO ⓥ

2 tbsp olive oil
2 shallots, finely chopped
75 ml/5 tbsp vegan white wine
250 g/1¼ cups Arborio rice
600 ml/2½ cups water
1 vegetable stock cube
4 tbsp any mix of chopped fresh
    herbs such as flat-leaf parsley,
    chives, oregano or marjoram
60 g/1½ cups chopped baby kale
40 g/1½ oz. vegetarian or vegan
    Parmesan cheese, finely grated
ground black pepper and finely
    grated lemon zest, to serve

Serves 4

A taste of spring in a risotto! Lots of fresh green herbs and sweet sautéed shallots combine to bring this vibrant risotto together.

Set the Instant pot to SAUTÉ. Add the oil to the pot then add the shallots and sauté for 3 minutes. Add the wine and stir for another 2 minutes then add the rice and stir. Pour in the water and crumble in the stock cube. Stir before closing the lid and setting to PRESSURE for 6 minutes. QPR at the end of cooking. Stir in the chopped herbs, kale and cheese.

Season generously with black pepper and sprinkle over some grated lemon zest to serve, if liked.

FRESH TOMATO RISOTTO

1 tbsp butter or olive oil
6 large tomatoes, diced
2 garlic cloves, chopped
250 g/1¼ cups Arborio rice
600 ml/2½ cups water
1 vegetable stock cube
2 tbsp grated vegetarian
    Parmesan cheese
30 g/1 cup torn fresh basil
½ tsp ground black pepper, plus
    extra to taste
fresh burrata cheese, to serve
    (optional)

Serves 4

The tomatoes in this recipe bring both sweetness and acidity to this fresh and summery risotto that is super quick and handy to make.

Set the Instant Pot to SAUTÉ. Add the butter or oil. Sauté the tomatoes, garlic and rice for about 2 minutes. Add the water and crumble in the stock cube. Set to PRESSURE for 6 minutes. QPR at the end of cooking and stir in the cheese, basil and black pepper. Check the seasoning and add more pepper as required.

Serve immediately topped with a dollop of soft burrata cheese, if liked.

CARROT & LEEK RISOTTO ⓥ

1 tbsp garlic-infused olive oil
1 leek, finely chopped
400 g/14 oz. carrots, finely
    chopped
200 ml/¾ cup carrot juice
400 ml/1¾ cups water
1 vegetable stock cube
grated zest of ½ a lemon
1 tbsp lemon juice
250 g/1¼ cups Arborio rice
50 g/2 oz. finely grated
    vegetarian or vegan Parmesan
    cheese
1 tbsp butter or vegan spread
a salad, to serve (optional)

Serves 4

*The clever use of carrot juice in this recipe brings
a fresh and zingy flavour to the risotto.*

Set the Instant Pot to SAUTÉ. Add the oil then sauté
the leek and carrots, stirring until the leeks are browning
slightly. Pour in the carrot juice and water and crumble in
the stock cube. Add the lemon zest and juice and then the
rice. Set to PRESSURE for 6 minutes. QPR at the end of
cooking and stir in the cheese and butter or vegan spread.
    Serve with a salad on the side, if liked.

FENNEL & FETA RISOTTO

1 tbsp oil
1 fennel bulb, diced
250 g/1¼ cups Arborio rice
75 ml/5 tbsp white wine
600 ml/2½ cups water
½ tsp salt
1 vegetable stock cube
2 tbsp chopped flat-leaf parsley
150 g/5½ oz. feta cheese,
    crumbled
2 tbsp butter
a salad, to serve (optional)

Serves 4

*A delightful combination of licoricey tasting fresh
fennel and salty feta cheese. The absence of onion
in this recipe makes for a change.*

Set the Instant Pot to SAUTÉ. Add the oil then sauté the
fennel for 4–5 minutes. Add the rice and stir, then add the
wine. Once the wine is starting to evaporate add the water
and salt and crumble in the stock cube. Set to PRESSURE
for 6 mins. QPR at the end of cooking and stir in the
parsley, feta and butter.
    Serve with a salad on the side, if liked.

1 tbsp olive oil
1 onion, chopped
1 carrot, coarsely grated
1 tsp each ground turmeric,
    ground cumin and garam
    masala
½ tsp chilli/chili paste
250 g/1¼ cups basmati rice
320 ml/scant 1⅓ cups water
1 x 400-g/14-oz. can chickpeas,
    drained and rinsed
1 vegetable stock cube
4 handfuls of baby spinach,
    washed
juice of 1 small lemon
1 tsp garlic-infused olive oil
    (optional)
chopped coriander/cilantro
    and lemon wedges, to serve
    (optional)

Serves 3–4

SPINACH, CARROT, CHICKPEA & LEMON PILAFF ⓥ

A light and vibrant rice dish, with lots of aromatic spices and just a little chilli/chili heat.

Set the Instant Pot to SAUTÉ and add the oil. When the oil is hot, add the onion and carrot and sauté for 3–5 minutes. Add all the spices, chilli/chili paste, rice, water and chickpeas and crumble in the stock cube. Set to RICE setting for 12 minutes. QPR at the end and stir in the spinach, lemon juice and garlic-infused olive oil (if using).

Serve with chopped coriander/cilantro scattered over the top and lemon wedges for squeezing, if liked.

---

2 tbsp olive oil
1 onion, chopped
2 garlic cloves, crushed
250 g/1¼ cups Arborio rice
75 ml/5 tbsp vegan white wine
170 g/6 oz. pepperdew peppers
    (drained weight) from a jar
10 cherry tomatoes, halved
200 g/7 oz. mushrooms, chopped
100 g/3½ oz. frozen green beans
1 x 400 g/14-oz. can chickpeas,
    drained and rinsed
1–2 tsp vegan paella spice mix or
    paella seasoning of your choice
1 tsp vegetable bouillon powder
600 ml/2½ cups water

Serves 4

VEGETABLE PAELLA ⓥ

This is such a cheat's meal. The best kind! All extremely easy-to-obtain ingredients and a straightforward method to follow. Enjoy this vegan version of the famous Spanish rice dish.

Set the Instant Pot to SAUTÉ and add the oil. When the oil is hot add the onion and sauté for about 3–5 minutes with the glass lid on. Add the garlic and rice and stir for 1 minute. Add the wine and stir for another minute. Add the pepperdew peppers, tomatoes, mushrooms, green beans and chickpeas, along with the paella spice mix, vegetable bouillon powder and water. Set to PRESSURE for 6 minutes then QPR.

Serve immediately.

MEDITERRANEAN RICE WITH HALLOUMI

1 tbsp garlic-infused olive oil plus 1 tbsp extra, for frying
2 celery sticks/stalks, finely chopped
3 carrots, finely chopped
2 courgettes/zucchini, cut into 3-cm/1¼-inch pieces
pinch of saffron threads
⅛ tsp each ground cumin and smoked paprika
¼ tsp dried oregano
250 g/1¼ cups basmati rice
320 ml/scant 1⅓ cups water
1 vegetable stock cube
100 g/¾ cup sun-blushed tomatoes, chopped
100 g/1 cup marinated artichoke hearts, chopped
2 x 225-g/8-oz. packs halloumi cheese, cut into cubes

Serves 4

Salty halloumi contrasts well with the fresh and zingy flavours and textures of this simple Mediterranean rice dish.

Set the Instant Pot to SAUTÉ and add the oil. Add the celery and carrots, and sauté with the glass lid on for 5 minutes. Add the courgettes/zucchini, saffron, cumin, paprika, oregano, rice and water, and crumble in the stock cube. Stir well. Set to RICE for 12 minutes and once cooked do a QPR. Stir in the tomatoes and artichokes then empty the rice out of the pot into bowls and keep warm.

Add the extra 1 tbsp garlic-infused olive oil to the pot and toss in the cubed halloumi. Stir until the cubes start to colour. Spoon the halloumi over the rice in the bowls and serve immediately.

EGG-FRIED VEGETABLE BROWN RICE

190 g/1 cup brown rice, rinsed
250 ml/1 cup water
1 tbsp oil
1 onion, chopped
1 large carrot, grated
1 garlic clove, chopped
100 g/¾ cup sweetcorn/corn (canned or frozen)
3 tbsp frozen green beans
1 tbsp soy sauce, plus extra to serve
4 eggs, beaten
finely sliced spring onions/ scallions, to serve

Serves 4

One of our family favourite meals is egg fried rice and this version is at the top of the list. The brown rice and egg combined with the saltiness from the soy sauce and sweetness from the vegetables make for a winning combination.

First cook the brown rice in the Instant Pot with the water. Set to PRESSURE for 15 minutes with 15 minutes NPR. Remove ALL the rice from the pot. Add the oil to the pot and set to SAUTÉ.

Add the onion and cook for about 3 minutes, then add the carrot and garlic and stir. Add the sweetcorn/corn and green beans and stir for another 2 minutes before adding the soy sauce and the cooked rice. Stir well then add the eggs and immediately turn off the heat and let them cook in the residual heat.

Serve with the sliced spring onions/scallions over the top and a drizzle of soy sauce, if liked.

CREAMY VEGETARIAN KEDGEREE

1 tbsp olive oil
1 orange (bell) pepper, chopped
1 courgette/zucchini, cubed
1 small onion, roughly chopped
½ tsp each ground turmeric and
    ground coriander
1 tsp mild curry powder
100 g/1 cup frozen peas
½ vegetable stock cube
250 g/1¼ cups basmati rice
320 ml/scant 1⅓ cups water
150 ml/⅔ cup crème fraîche
salt and ground black pepper,
    to season
4 hard-boiled/cooked eggs and
    chopped flat-leaf parsley,
    to serve

Serves 4

One of the family favourite recipes from my first Instant Pot cookbook is the kedgeree. However, as we move to eat more vegetarian and vegan meals as a family this version has become a favourite alternative.

Set the Instant Pot to SAUTÉ and add the oil. Add the (bell) pepper, courgette/zucchini and onion and sauté for about 5 minutes. Add the spices and curry powder, followed by the peas and stir. Crumble in the stock cube, add the rice and water and stir again. Place the lid on the pot and secure. Set to RICE for 12 minutes. Use a QPR at the end of cooking.

Stir in the crème fraîche and season to taste. Serve with the hard-boiled/cooked eggs, peeled, rinsed and quartered, and a sprinkle of chopped flat-leaf parsley.

LEEK, PEA & HALLOUMI QUINOTTO

2 tbsp butter or vegan spread
1 large leek, sliced and washed
170 g/1 cup quinoa
2 tsp vegetable bouillon powder
250 ml/1 cup water
180 g/scant 1½ cups frozen peas
2 tbsp each chopped mint and
  flat-leaf parsley, plus extra
  to serve
1 x 225-g/8-oz. pack halloumi
  cheese, sliced or cut into
  triangles (as shown) and pan
  fried in a little oil until brown
  on both sides

Serves 2-3

A quinotto is simply a risotto-style dish but made using quinoa instead of Arborio or risotto rice. This refreshing and spring-like combination of leeks, peas and herbs with slices of salty halloumi cheese is ideal for a quick lunch.

Put the butter or spread into the Instant Pot and heat on SAUTÉ. Add the leek and sauté until the edges start to brown a little. Add the quinoa, vegetable bouillon powder, and water, and give everything a good stir. Set to PRESSURE for 2 minutes. NPR at the end of cooking, then stir in the peas and herbs until the peas have defrosted.

Scatter the extra flat-leaf parsley and mint over the top and add the pan-fried halloumi slices to serve.

QUINOA TABBOULEH WITH FETA

170 g/1 cup quinoa
300 ml/1¼ cups vegetable stock
1 large cucumber, finely diced
1 celery stick/stalk, finely diced
1 red onion, finely diced
2 tbsp each chopped mint and
  flat-leaf parsley
2 tbsp toasted pine nuts
2 tbsp olive oil
grated zest of ½ a lemon
2 tbsp lemon juice
200 g/7 oz. feta cheese, crumbled
salt and ground black pepper,
  to taste

Serves 4

This delicately refreshing, herby dish is bolstered by the beautifully tart and salty feta cheese.

Put the quinoa in the Instant Pot and pour in the vegetable stock. Set to PRESSURE for 2 minutes and NPR at the end of cooking. Once the quinoa is cooked and pressure released, fluff it up with a fork and leave the pressure cooker off whilst the quinoa cools. Once cooled, stir in all the remaining ingredients, keeping a little feta back to serve, and season to taste.

Scatter the reserved feta over the top and serve.

PASTA

VEGAN TEMPEH BOLOGNESE Ⓥ

1 tbsp olive oil
1 onion, chopped
2 carrots, chopped
220 g/8 oz. mushrooms, chopped
2 garlic cloves, chopped
1 tbsp vegan Worcester sauce
2 tbsp tomato purée/paste
1 tsp dried oregano
1 tsp balsamic vinegar
1 tsp maple syrup
1 tbsp vegetable bouillon powder
300 g/3½ cups brown rice penne
1 x 400-g/14 oz. can chopped
    tomatoes
600 ml/2½ cups water
175 g/6½ oz. tempeh, chopped
salt and ground black pepper,
    to season
grated vegan Parmesan cheese,
    to serve

Serves 3–4

Tempeh is made from fermented soybeans. It comes in a bar or small bars that can be eaten as is but this recipe provides a great way of using tempeh to give both texture and flavour to a well-known pasta dish.

Set the Instant Pot to SAUTÉ. Heat the oil and sauté the onion and carrots for 3–5 minutes then add the mushrooms and garlic. After another 3 minutes add all of the remaining ingredients. Set to PRESSURE for 4 minutes (or half the cooking time stated on the penne packaging plus 1 minute). QPR at the end of cooking.

Season to taste and serve with grated cheese sprinkled over the top.

VEGAN VEGGIE PASTA Ⓥ

1 tbsp oil
1 onion, chopped
2 celery sticks/stalks, finely
    chopped
2 red (bell) peppers, chopped
300 g/3½ cups brown rice penne
1 vegetable stock cube
400 ml/1¾ cups water
350 g/1½ cups passata (Italian
    strained tomatoes)
2 tbsp nutritional yeast flakes
1 tsp dried oregano or marjoram
2 medium sweet potatoes, cut
    into 2-cm/¾-inch cubes

Serves 3–4

This recipe uses nutritional yeast flakes to give a creamy, umami feel and taste to this quick and easy veg-packed pasta dish.

Set the Instant Pot to SAUTÉ. Heat the oil then add the onion, celery and (bell) peppers. Once the onions are soft add all the remaining ingredients except the sweet potatoes and give it all a good stir to make sure as much of the penne as possible is under the liquid. Add the sweet potatoes on top. Set the pot to PRESSURE for 3 minutes (or half the cooking time stated on the pasta packaging plus 1 minute). QPR at the end of cooking then stir well before serving.

SPAGHETTI WITH COURGETTE & LEMON Ⓥ

350 g/12 oz. brown rice spaghetti
grated zest of 1 lemon
2 tbsp chopped flat-leaf parsley
2 tsp vegetable bouillon powder
650 ml/2¾ cups water, plus
    150 ml/⅔ cup (divided)
1 tbsp butter or vegan spread
2 courgettes/zucchini, cut into
    strips using a vegetable peeler
salt and ground black pepper,
    to season
grated vegan Parmesan cheese
    and chopped mint, to serve

Serves 3-4

A fresh and zingy vegan pasta dish made with light, summery ingredients.

Put the spaghetti, lemon zest, parsley, vegetable bouillon powder and 650 ml/2¾ cups water into the Instant Pot. Set to PRESSURE for 3 minutes (or half the cooking time stated on the spaghetti packaging plus 1 minute). QPR at the end of cooking. Open the lid and stir well. As spaghetti can stick together add the butter or spread and another 150 ml/⅔ cup water and set to SAUTÉ. Stir in the courgettes/zucchini and stir until the spaghetti is cooked through and separated.

    Season to taste and serve with grated cheese and chopped mint sprinkled over the top.

3-INGREDIENT TOMATO PASTA Ⓥ

200 g/3 cups brown rice fusilli
400 g/14-oz. can tomato soup
    (choose a vegan version if
    you prefer)
400 ml/1¾ cups water
2 tbsp nutritional yeast flakes

Serves 2-3

Quite frankly there are evenings when I can barely be bothered to cook a meal. After an exhausting day at work what could be easier than a recipe that requires you to put three ingredients (plus some water) into the pot and press a few buttons then come back to a bowl of delicious pasta.

Put all the ingredients into the Instant Pot. Set to PRESSURE for 3 minutes (or half the cooking time stated on the fusilli packaging plus 1 minute). Use a QPR at the end of cooking. Give everything a good stir and serve. It's as easy as that!

PASTA WITH BUTTERNUT SQUASH & SAGE SAUCE Ⓥ

2 tbsp vegan spread or butter
1 red onion, finely chopped
2 garlic cloves, chopped
3 fresh sage leaves, chopped
350 g/12 oz. butternut squash, cut into cubes
750 ml/3 cups water
1 vegetable stock cube
300 g/3½ cups brown rice fusilli
1 tsp smoked paprika
50 g/2 oz. vegan or vegetarian Parmesan cheese, grated
100 ml/6 tbsp oat cream or dairy cream
salt and ground black pepper, to season
fried sage leaves, to serve (optional)

Serves 3–4

The combination of sweet, sautéed red onion, garlic and sage with sweet and creamy butternut squash brings out the best in this one-pot pasta meal.

Set the Instant Pot to SAUTÉ. Add the vegan spread or butter to the inner pot then once melted add the onion and sauté for 3 minutes before adding the garlic and sage. Sauté for a further 2 minutes. Add the squash and water and crumble in the stock cube. Stir then seal the lid and set to PRESSURE for 4 minutes. Use QPR at the end of this time then open the lid and mash the squash in the pot with a potato masher.

Add the fusilli and paprika, stir and make sure the pasta is submerged. Replace the lid and set to PRESSURE for 3 minutes (or half the cooking time stated on the fusilli packaging plus 1 minute). QPR once again at the end of cooking and stir in the cheese and cream.

Season to taste and serve with fried sage leaves scattered over the top, if liked.

CREAMY CHEESE & SPINACH PASTA

1 tbsp butter
1 tsp garlic powder
½ tsp smoked paprika
200 g/3 cups brown rice fusilli
450 ml/scant 2 cups water
30 g/2 oz. vegetarian Parmesan cheese, grated
180 g/6 oz. vegetarian Cheddar cheese, grated
130 g/2 cups chopped fresh spinach
salt and ground black pepper, to season
chopped flat-leaf parsley, to serve

Serves 2–3

A decadent and indulgent vegetarian pasta dish with just a little bit of green!

Put the butter, garlic powder, smoked paprika, fusilli and water in the Instant Pot. Cook on PRESSURE for 3 minutes (or half the cooking time stated on the fusilli packaging plus 1 minute) with QPR at the end of cooking. Open the lid and stir in both the cheeses and spinach until combined.

Season to taste and scatter the chopped flat-leaf parsley over the top to serve.

SUN-BLUSHED TOMATO & LENTIL PASTA Ⓥ

1 tbsp olive oil

1 courgette/zucchini, cut into 5-mm/¼-inch slices

1 onion, chopped

2 garlic cloves, chopped

1 tbsp tomato purée/paste

1 tbsp balsamic vinegar

1 tsp salt

½ tsp dried marjoram

300 g/2½ cups brown rice penne

700 ml/scant 3 cups water

70 g/1 cup sun-blushed tomatoes, chopped

1 x 400-g/14-oz. can brown lentils, drained and rinsed

salt and ground black pepper, to taste

crumbled feta cheese or sliced artichokes and chopped fresh oregano, to serve (optional)

Serves 3–4

A filling, wholesome, tomato-based pasta and lentil one-pot dish with optional feta cheese.

Set the Instant Pot to SAUTÉ and heat the oil. Sauté the courgette/zucchini for about 5 minutes until softening slightly and starting to brown then remove from the pot. Add the onion and garlic and stir quickly for a couple of minutes before adding the tomato purée/paste, vinegar, salt and marjoram, and stirring rapidly. Press CANCEL then add the penne and water, and give everything a good stir. Pop the sun-blushed tomatoes on top and set the pot to PRESSURE for 4 minutes (or half the cooking time stated on the penne packaging plus 1 minute). QPR at the end of cooking. Add the courgette/zucchini to the pot, stir in the lentils until warmed through and season to taste.

Serve with feta or sliced artichokes (for a vegan option) and chopped fresh oregano over the top, if liked.

GARLIC MUSHROOM PASTA Ⓥ

1 tbsp olive oil

250 g/9 oz. sliced mushrooms

2 tbsp chopped garlic

200 g/2 cups brown rice penne

½ tsp dried marjoram

1 vegetable stock cube

450 ml/scant 2 cups water

50 g/2 oz. vegetarian or vegan Parmesan cheese, grated

chopped flat-leaf parsley, to serve

Serves 2–3

Classic and complementary flavours combine in this simple and quick pasta dish.

Set the Instant Pot to SAUTÉ and add the oil. Add the mushrooms and sauté for 5 minutes then stir in the garlic. After 1 minute add the penne and marjoram, crumble in the stock cube then add the water (or sufficient) to just cover the pasta. Cook on PRESSURE for 3 minutes (or half the time stated on the penne packaging plus 1 minute) with QPR at the end of cooking. Open the lid and press CANCEL then SAUTÉ and add the cheese. Stir until the sauce is the consistency you'd like.

Serve the pasta with parsley sprinkled over the top.

EGGS & CHEESE

CLASSIC CAULIFLOWER CHEESE

600 g/21 oz. cauliflower, cut into
   4-cm/1¹/₂-inch wide florets
125 ml/¹/₂ cup water
2 tbsp butter
2 tbsp plain/all-purpose flour
250 ml/1 cup milk
200 g/7 oz. mature/sharp
   vegetarian Cheddar cheese,
   grated
¹/₂ tsp salt
¹/₂ tsp garlic powder

Serves 4

Here is a wonderfully consistent way to create this easy, cheesy dish.

Place the cauliflower in the Instant Pot with the water. Set to PRESSURE for 2 minutes and do a QPR at the end of cooking.

Drain the cauliflower and place in a shallow baking dish. Press SAUTÉ and melt the butter then add the flour, stirring rapidly until you have a paste. Add the milk slowly, stirring constantly. This will thicken quickly so as soon as all the milk is added stir in the cheese then the salt and garlic powder. Immediately pour the cheese sauce over the cauliflower in the baking dish. Place under a preheated grill/broiler set to medium and cook until the sauce starts to brown on top.

Serve immediately.

CAULIFLOWER CHEESE SOUP

1 tbsp butter or olive oil
1 onion, chopped
¹/₂ tsp mustard powder
1 large cauliflower, broken into
   florets
650 ml/2³/₄ cups water
1 vegetable stock cube
100 g/¹/₂ cup cream cheese
100 g/3¹/₂ oz. mature/sharp
   vegetarian Cheddar cheese,
   grated
ground black pepper, to taste

Serves 4

Cauliflower cheese is an extremely popular way to enjoy this vegetable. And this soup is a very comforting way to enjoy cauliflower cheese.

Set the Instant Pot to SAUTÉ. Add the butter or oil then once hot add the onion and sauté for 3 minutes. Add the mustard powder and stir. Then add the cauliflower and water and crumble in the stock cube. Set to PRESSURE for 4 minutes. QPR at the end of cooking and stir in the cream cheese and grated Cheddar. Blend using a stick blender or food processor.

Season to taste with black pepper and serve.

LEEK & CAERPHILLY CHEESE SOUP

1 tbsp butter
3 leeks, cut lengthways then
    sliced horizontally
1 large baking potato, peeled
    and cut into 3-cm/1¼-inch
    cubes
500 ml/2 cups vegetable stock
100 g/3½ oz. Caerphilly cheese
    (or Wensleydale cheese),
    crumbled, plus extra to serve
100 ml/6 tbsp crème fraîche
toasted and chopped hazelnuts
    and snipped chives, to serve
    (optional)

Serves 4

Leeks and Caerphilly cheese are synonymous with Wales which is where I first tasted a version of this soup. The key to making this soup is to ensure the leeks are lightly caramelized before adding the other ingredients. That way, the sweet leeks and crumbly Caerphilly cheese contrast with great results.

Set the Instant Pot to SAUTÉ and melt the butter. Add the leeks and sauté until they are starting to caramelize. Add the cubed potato and pour in the stock. Set to PRESSURE for 10 minutes. Do a QPR at the end of cooking. Once cooled slightly blend using a stick blender or food processor. Reheat the soup in the pot on SAUTÉ then stir in the cheese and crème fraîche.

Serve with extra crumbled cheese, toasted hazelnuts and snipped chives over the top, if liked.

CHEESY ENCHILADA RICE SOUP

1 tbsp olive oil
1 onion, chopped
2 celery sticks/stalks, chopped
350 ml/1⅓ cups enchilada sauce
600 ml/2½ cups water
1 tsp salt
1 tsp ground cumin
1 tsp garlic powder
juice of 1 lime
200 g/1 cup brown rice, rinsed
150 g/5½ oz. mature/sharp
    vegetarian Cheddar cheese,
    grated
sliced avocado, to serve (optional)

Serves 4

This is a wholesome Mexican-inspired soup. It is a particularly substantial soup thanks to the brown rice and cheese components.

Set the Instant Pot to SAUTÉ and heat the oil. Once hot add the onion and celery, and sauté for 5 minutes. Add all other remaining ingredients (except the cheese and avocado), stir well then set to PRESSURE for 25 minutes. QPR at the end of cooking and stir in the cheese.

Serve with avocado slices on top, if liked.

FETA, PEA & MINT CRUSTLESS QUICHES

4 eggs
70 ml/5 tbsp milk
70 g/2½ oz. vegetarian Parmesan
  cheese, grated
1 garlic clove, crushed (optional)
40 g/⅓ cup frozen peas
40 g/1½ oz. feta cheese,
  crumbled
1 tbsp chopped mint, plus extra
  leaves to serve
salt and ground black pepper,
  to season

4 x individual ramekins (that
  fit into your Instant Pot when
  placed on the trivet), oiled

Serves 4

*This is ideal for a quick breakfast when you want
something to keep your energy levels up for hours,
or a light supper at the end of a long day.*

Add the eggs, milk, Parmesan and garlic (if using) to a
mixing bowl and whisk to combine. Stir in the peas, feta
and chopped mint and season. Pour the mixture into the
prepared ramekins. Pour 500 ml/2 cups water into the
Instant Pot then pop the trivet on top. Carefully place the
filled ramekins onto the trivet. Set to PRESSURE for
15 minutes with QPR at the end of cooking. The quiches
will be quite risen when you open the lid but will fall back
a little when served.

   Serve hot or cold, as preferred, in the ramekins with
mint scattered over the top, if liked.

EMMENTAL, RED PEPPER & TOMATO CRUSTLESS QUICHES

4 eggs
¼ red (bell) pepper, finely diced
6 cherry tomatoes, finely diced
50 ml/3½ tbsp single cream
55 g/2 oz. grated Emmental
  cheese
salt and ground black pepper,
  to season

4 x individual ramekins (that
  fit into your Instant Pot when
  placed on the trivet), oiled

Serves 4

*A light and bright grain-free quiche served in four
individual portions. A quick and easy meal that can
cook whilst you are busy elsewhere!*

Add all the ingredients to a mixing bowl, whisk to combine
and season. Pour the mixture into the prepared ramekins.
Pour 500 ml/2 cups water into the Instant Pot then pop
the trivet on top. Carefully place the filled ramekins on top
of the trivet. Set to PRESSURE for 15 minutes then QPR at
the end of cooking. The quiches will be quite risen when
you open the lid but will fall back a little when served.

   Serve hot or cold, as preferred, in the ramekins.

'BAKED' CAMEMBERT

1 x whole vegetarian Camembert
   cheese
a few sprigs of thyme
1 tsp honey
a selection of freshly prepared
   crudités of your choice, i.e.
   sliced carrots, (bell) peppers,
   radishes, chicory/endive and
   celery or fresh apple

Serves 4 as an appetizer

Thanks to Maria from www.feistytapas.com not only for this simple and effective way of preparing a whole Camembert, but also for introducing me to the Instant Pot in the first place.

Unwrap the cheese, add some sprigs of thyme to the top and drizzle over the honey then rewrap the whole cheese completely in greaseproof/parchment paper.

Add 250 ml/1 cup water to the Instant Pot. Place the trivet in the pot and then add the wrapped cheese on top. Set to PRESSURE for 10 minutes. Leave to NPR for 10 minutes before releasing the pressure.

Remove and unwrap the cheese. Wipe away any excess water with paper towels, slice open the rind of the cheese to reveal the molten cheese beneath and serve immediately with the crudités of your choice.

PERFECT SOFT-BOILED EGGS

up to 6 fresh eggs, medium size
500 ml/2 cups water

A deliciously runny yolk, every time! These make a light meal on toast or a protein-rich addition to many of the rice or quinoa-based dishes in this book.

Put the water in the Instant Pot and add the trivet. Pop the eggs on the trivet and set to 3 minutes on LOW PRESSURE. That means setting to PRESSURE then adjusting to LOW. QPR at the end of cooking. Immediately remove the eggs from the pot and place in cold water for 30 seconds before peeling, rinsing and serving as desired.

BRIE & CIDER RISOTTO

1 tbsp olive oil
250 g/9 oz. mushrooms, sliced
2 garlic cloves, crushed
100 ml/6 tbsp hard cider
250 g/1¼ cups Arborio rice
1 vegetable stock cube
1 tbsp chopped flat-leaf parsley,
    plus extra to serve
600 ml/2½ cups water
1 x 125-g/4½-oz. vegetarian Brie,
    cut into cubes (you can leave
    the rind on if you like)
ground black pepper, to season
a bitterleaf green salad, to serve
    (optional)

Serves 4

*Having spent a year of my life in Normandy, France,
the combination of cider and cheese is one that is
extremely familiar and comforting to me. This is quite
a rich dish and one that we tend to enjoy in the colder
months. We serve this with a bitter leaf green salad.*

Set the Instant Pot to SAUTÉ and add the oil. Sauté the
mushrooms and garlic until the mushrooms release their
liquid then add the cider. Once it has mostly evaporated
add the rice and stir well. Crumble in the stock cube and
add 600 ml/2½ cups water. Secure the lid in place then
set to PRESSURE for 6 minutes. Use QPR at the end of
cooking. Stir in the Brie until melted, along with the
flat-leaf parsley.

Serve with chopped flat-leaf parsley and a few grinds
of black pepper over the top and a bitterleaf salad on the
side, if liked.

HALLOUMI, CHICKPEAS &
PRESERVED LEMONS

1 tbsp olive oil
1 onion, chopped
1 x 225-g/9-oz. pack halloumi
    cheese, cut into cubes
½ tsp ground turmeric
2 tsp chopped mint
3 garlic cloves, chopped
400 g/14 oz. baby spinach
1 x 400-g/14-oz. can chickpeas,
    drained and rinsed
2 preserved lemons, diced
salt and ground black pepper,
    to taste
chopped flat-leaf parsley,
    to serve

Serves 2

*A delightful mix of creamy, salty halloumi cheese
and tart preserved lemons.*

Set the Instant Pot to SAUTÉ and heat the oil. Add the
onions and halloumi and sauté until the halloumi has some
colour on the outside. Add all the remaining ingredients,
stir, then set to PRESSURE for 1 minute. QPR at the end
of cooking. Stir again and season to taste.

Serve with chopped flat-leaf parsley scattered over
the top.

MEDITERRANEAN GOATS' CHEESE, LENTIL & SWEET POTATO PIES

1 tbsp garlic-infused olive oil

1 onion, roughly chopped

2 celery sticks/stalks, chopped

1 yellow (bell) pepper, chopped

1 large sweet potato, peeled and cut into 1-cm/½-inch cubes (300 g/10½ oz. peeled weight)

200 g/¾ cup passata (Italian strained tomatoes)

½ tsp dried oregano

2 tbsp tapenade (olive paste)

1 x 400-g/14 oz. can green lentils drained

1 x 280-g/10 oz. sheet ready-to-use puff pastry (gluten-free if liked)

1 x 200-g/7-oz. soft goats' cheese log

1 tbsp milk, to glaze

4 x mini pie dishes for cooking the pies IN THE OVEN after the pie mixture has been prepared in your Instant Pot (if you like, you can use oblong, rolled edge foil pie dishes, roughly 13 x 11 cm/5 x 4¼ inch with a 3-cm/1¼-inch depth)

Serves 4

These flavour-packed savoury pies are a real comfort. The meltingly soft lentils and squash combined with a crisp pastry top make for a delicious vegetarian treat.

Set the Instant Pot to SAUTÉ then add the oil. Once hot add the onion, celery and (bell) pepper, and sauté until the vegetables are softening. Add the sweet potato, passata, oregano and tapenade. Deglaze the pan and give everything a good stir. Place the green lentils on top of the other ingredients. Set to PRESSURE for 3 minutes with a QPR at the end of cooking.

Meanwhile, prepare the pastry pie tops. Lay the sheet of pastry out flat. Use a sharp knife to cut four pieces of equal size using an upturned pie dish as a template. (You might also like to make some designs from the excess pastry to top the pies with so reserve it.)

Preheat the oven to 180°C fan/200°C/400°F/Gas 6.

Divide the contents of the Instant Pot into the pie dishes. Dot the goats' cheese over the top of each pie then place the pastry pie top (and any decoration) on top and cut a small slit in the pastry to allow for steam to be released. Use a pastry brush to apply a thin layer of milk to the surface of each one. Bake in the preheated oven for about 20 minutes, until golden brown on top.

Allow to cool slightly before serving and take care as the contents may still be very hot.

SIDE DISHES

PERFECT BEETROOT ⓥ

**500 g/18 oz. choose beetroot/
beets between 2.5–5 cm/1–2
inches in diameter i.e. small (if
your beetroot/beets are larger
you'll need to cut them to
this size)**

**250 ml/1 cup water
preserve in apple cider vinegar,
to serve (optional)**

a large, sterlized, sealable jar
(optional)

Serves 4 as a side

*Cooking beetroot/beets on the hob/stovetop is often
a frustrating task. It takes forever and the pot tends to
run dry of water too quickly. Pressure cooking is far
easier and more consistent.*

Put 250 ml/1 cup water in base of the Instant Pot and pop
in the trivet. Place the rinsed beetroots/beets (whole or
chopped to size) on the trivet and set to PRESSURE for
20 minutes. NPR at the end of cooking.

Serve immediately as desired or slice and preserve
in apple cider vinegar to enjoy another time, as preferred.

MUSHY PEAS ⓥ

1 x 110-g/4-oz. potato, chopped
   into 2-cm/³/₄-inch cubes
100 ml/6 tbsp water (divided)
300 g/2¼ cups frozen peas
¼ tsp salt

Serves 4 as a side

There are many ways to make mushy peas, a good old-fashioned British staple. I prefer using frozen peas for their bright green colour and fresh flavour. This is a vegan version of mushy peas and is such a delicious side dish.

Place the potato and 50 ml/3 tbsp water in the Instant Pot and set to PRESSURE for 3 minutes. QPR at the end of cooking. Add the peas, the remaining water and the salt to the pot. Set to PRESSURE for 1 minute then QPR again. Use a stick blender or food processor to process the peas to the consistency of mushy peas. You should still be able to see flecks of pea skin in the mixture. Serve as desired.

PERFECT GREEN BEANS ⓥ

300 g/10½ oz. green beans,
   trimmed and rinsed
125 ml/½ cup water
extra virgin olive oil and sea salt,
   to serve (optional)

Serves 4 as a side

It's not always easy to get green beans cooked to perfection. This is such an easy method to achieve great results every time.

Place the beans and water in the Instant Pot. Set to LOW PRESSURE for 2 minutes. This means pressing PRESSURE then adjusting to LOW. QPR at the end of cooking. Dress with extra virgin olive oil and sea salt, if liked, and serve.

REFRIED BEANS ⓥ

240 g/1⅓ cups dried pinto beans
1 litre/4 cups water
1 tsp salt, plus extra to season
2 tbsp butter or vegan spread
    plus 1 tbsp (optional) for the
    best consistency
1 onion, chopped
salt and ground black pepper,
    to season
chopped coriander/cilantro and
    lime wedges, to serve (optional)

Serves 6 as a side

These creamy and wholesome beans are traditionally served with Mexican-style dishes.

Soak the beans in the water for at least 4 hours (this can be done in the Instant Pot with the lid on and set to DELAYED START) then set the pot to PRESSURE for 20 minutes. NPR at the end of cooking. Drain the beans but reserve 125 ml/½ cup of the cooking water.

Set the Instant Pot pot to SAUTÉ and add the butter or vegan spread and onion. Once the onion is soft stir in the cooked beans. Transfer the buttery beans to a food processor with 90 ml/generous ⅓ cup of the reserved bean cooking water. Blend until they're the right texture. Add a little more of the reserved water and butter or vegan spread if you like them creamier, and check the seasoning before serving in a bowl topped with chopped coriander/cilantro and lime wedges, if liked.

MEXICAN SPICY RICE ⓥ

2 tsp olive oil
2 onions, sliced
3 large flat mushrooms, sliced
10 cherry tomatoes, halved
¾ tsp smoked paprika
½ tsp ground cumin
1 tsp chilli/chili paste
1 tbsp tomato purée/paste
1 vegetable stock cube
250 g/1¼ cups basmati rice
320 ml/scant 1⅓ cups water
1 x 400-g/14-oz. can black
    beans, drained and rinsed
grated vegan cheese and Vegan
    Sour Cream (see page 11),
    to serve (optional)

Serves 4 as a side

A satisfying vegetable-rich dish combining rice with black beans for a traditional Mexican experience.

Set the Instant Pot to SAUTÉ and add the oil. Sauté the onions for 5 minutes, stirring occasionally. Add the mushrooms and sauté for a further 3 minutes then the tomatoes for a further 1 minute. Add all the remaining ingredients (except the black beans) and stir well. Set to RICE for 12 minutes and do a QPR at the end of cooking. Open the lid then stir the black beans through the rice until warmed through.

Serve topped with a good dollop of Vegan Sour Cream and grated vegan cheese, if liked.

HOMEMADE BAKED BEANS ⓥ

1 tbsp oil
1 onion, chopped
2 x 400-g/14-oz. cans haricot/
   navy beans, drained and rinsed
450 g/2 cups passata (Italian
   strained tomatoes)
1 tbsp maple syrup
1/2 tsp blackstrap molasses or
   black treacle
1/2 tsp smoked paprika
1/2 tsp salt
sourdough toast, to serve
   (optional)

Serves 4 as a side

A staple in our household. You can save so much money by making your own and you even have the choice to make them your own with your desired level of sweetness and spiciness.

Set the Instant Pot to to SAUTÉ and add the oil then the onion. Sauté for about 5 minutes then add all the remaining ingredients. Set to PRESSURE for 2 minutes then allow an NPR at the end of cooking before serving.

Serve in the traditional way spooned over hot toasted sourdough bread, if liked, or enjoy as a side dish.

CREAMY MASHED POTATOES ⓥ

250 ml/1 cup water
5 x 160–240-g/6–8-oz. potatoes,
   peeled and cut into 40–60-g/
   1 1/2–2-oz. wedges
100 ml/6 tbsp any milk of
   your choice
3 tbsp butter or vegan spread
salt and ground white pepper,
   to season

Serves 4 as a side

A dish that is so easy to make consistently the same way, and to the same standard in the Instant Pot using this method, that it deserves inclusion in this book.

Pour the water into the Instant Pot. Place the vegetable steamer in the pot and add the potatoes in the steamer trivet. Close the lid and cook at PRESSURE for 8 minutes. Allow NPR for 5 minutes then release the remaining pressure. Remove the lid, discard the water then mash the cooked potatoes in the pot with the milk and butter or vegan spread, seasoning as you go. Continue to mash and season until you are happy with both the consistency and flavour before serving.

INSTANT RATATOUILLE ⓥ

600 g/21 oz. total weight a mix
    of frozen ratatouille vegetables
    i.e. tomatoes, (bell) peppers,
    aubergine/eggplant, courgette/
    zucchini and onions
1 x 200-g/7-oz. can chopped
    tomatoes
1 tsp balsamic vinegar
1/2 tsp vegan Worcester Sauce
1/2 tsp soy sauce
salt and ground black pepper,
    to taste
basil leaves and Wholewheat
    Couscous (see recipe below),
    to serve (optional)

Serves 4 as a side

Keeping frozen vegetable mixes for emergencies is something I learnt as a student and all these years on I can still be surprised by what delicious meals can be created with some frozen mixed vegetables and very few added ingredients.

Put all of the ingredients into the Instant Pot and set to PRESSURE for 4 minutes. Allow an NPR at the end of cooking.

    Season the ratatouille to taste, top with a sprinkle of chopped basil and serve as desired.

WHOLEWHEAT COUSCOUS ⓥ

2 tbsp butter or vegan spread
330 g/scant 2 cups wholewheat
    couscous
1 tsp salt
800 ml/3 1/3 cups water
chopped flat-leaf parsley and
    lemon slices, to serve (optional)

Serves 6 as a side

Light, fluffy and 'buttery' couscous is such a great accompaniment to any Mediterranean or Middle Eastern-style dish.

Set the Instant Pot to SAUTÉ and melt the butter or spread then immediately stir in the couscous and salt. Press CANCEL then add the water and stir well. Secure the lid in place then set to PRESSURE for 5 minutes. QPR at the end of cooking and stir again.

    Top with chopped parsley and add lemon slices to serve, if liked.

RED PEPPER HUMMUS Ⓥ

170 g/1 cup dried chickpeas, soaked for 8 hours

FOR THE HUMMUS
340 g/2¼ cups cooked chickpeas (see above)
230 g/8 oz. roasted red (bell) peppers from a jar, very well drained and chopped
juice of ½ a lemon
2 tbsp tahini
1 garlic clove, crushed
1½ tbsp olive oil
1 tsp salt
1 tsp ground cumin
chopped flat-leaf parsley and smoked paprika, to garnish
selection of freshly prepared vegetable crudités (see page 100) and toasted pitta bread, to serve (optional)

Makes 6-8 servings

This healthy recipe creates a sweet, bright orange hummus with red (bell) pepper added for flavour and texture, but also meaning less oil is needed.

Place the soaked chickpeas in the Instant Pot with 1 litre/ 4 cups fresh water. Cook on PRESSURE for 15 minutes with NPR at the end of cooking. Drain. This will yield roughly 340 g/2¼ cups cooked chickpeas.

To make the hummus, combine the specified amount of cooked chickpeas with all the other ingredients (except the parsley) in a food processor until smooth.

Serve with chopped parsley and a dusting of paprika over the top and crudités and toasted pitta bread on the side for dipping, if liked.

GREEK SPLIT YELLOW PEA & GARLIC PURÉE Ⓥ

220 g/heaped 1 cup yellow split peas, rinsed
1 onion, roughly chopped
1½ tbsp chopped garlic
2 bay leaves
1 tsp dried marjoram or oregano
600 ml/2½ cups water
2½ tsp vegetable bouillon powder
35 ml/2½ tbsp extra virgin olive oil
juice of 1 lemon
ground black pepper, to taste
toasted pitta bread, to serve

Makes 6-8 servings

This delicious Greek dip can be served with garnishes such as capers, sun-blushed tomatoes, feta cheese or caramelized onions over the top.

Place the split peas, onion, garlic, bay leaves, herbs, water and bouillon powder in the Instant Pot. Set to PRESSURE for 10 minutes with QPR at the end of cooking. Add the olive oil and lemon juice season generously with black pepper. Process to a smooth purée using a food processor or stick blender.

Serve warm with all or any of the suggested toppings (see introduction), if liked, and toasted pitta bread to dip.

VEGETABLE PILAFF Ⓥ

1 tbsp oil
1 onion, chopped
3 carrots, cut into roughly
   1-cm/½-inch cubes
2 garlic cloves, chopped
1 tsp salt
1 tsp ground cumin
¼ tsp ground turmeric
250 g/1¼ cups basmati rice
320 ml/scant 1⅓ cups water
75 g/heaped ½ cup roasted and
   salted cashew nuts
1 tbsp chopped coriander/
   cilantro, plus extra to serve
4 tbsp any unflavoured yogurt of
   your choice
2 tsp harissa paste mixed with
   1 tbsp water

Serves 4 as a side

The yellow from the turmeric and the orange carrots make for a visually appealing and delicious rice side dish. This is called 'yellow rice' in our household.

Set the Instant Pot to SAUTÉ. Add the oil, onion and carrots and sauté for about 5 minutes. Add the garlic, salt and spices before adding the rice and water and stirring again. Set to RICE for 12 minutes and QPR at the end of cooking. Add the coriander/cilantro and cashew nuts and stir in.

Mix the yogurt with the harissa paste and water mixture. Drizzle over the pilaff and scatter over some chopped coriander/cilantro to serve, if liked.

'BUTTERY' BROWN BASMATI RICE Ⓥ

190 g/heaped 1 cup brown
   basmati rice
250 ml/1 cup water
2 tbsp butter or vegan spread

Serves 4 as a side

Inspired by my teenage daughter who loves brown rice and in fact prefers it to white rice but claims butter or vegan spread mixed through is an absolute must!

Put the rice and water in the Instant Pot. Set to PRESSURE for 15 minutes. NPR for 15 minutes then QPR. Finally, stir in the butter or vegan spread and serve immediately.

SWEET THINGS & DRINKS

STRAWBERRY CHIA COMPÔTE Ⓥ

**500 g/2¼ cups frozen
    strawberries**
3 tbsp honey or maple syrup
2 tbsp chia seeds

Makes 10 servings

*A subtly tart, pleasantly sweet compôte that is ideal for serving
over yogurt or in your morning porridge.*

Put the strawberries and honey or maple syrup in the Instant Pot.
Set to PRESSURE for 3 minutes. NPR at the end of cooking. Add the
chia seeds and then process in a food processor once cool enough.

Leave to cool further then store in a sealable container in the
fridge and use as required.

RHUBARB COMPÔTE Ⓥ

**400 g/14 oz. rhubarb, rinsed and
    chopped into 4-cm/1½-inch
    pieces**
60 ml/4 tbsp orange juice
**3–4 tbsp honey or maple syrup,
    to taste**

Makes 4-6 servings

*Is it a fruit? Is it a vegetable? Either way it tastes delicious
when combined with the natural sweetness of orange juice and
maple syrup. This compôte is ideal for dolloping over yogurt.*

Put all the ingredients into the Instant Pot. Set to PRESSURE
for 2 minutes. Do an NPR at the end of cooking. Stir a fork through
the pot to loosen the rhubarb into a compôte consistency.

Leave to cool further then store in a sealable container in the
fridge and use as required.

APPLE PURÉE Ⓥ

**6 eating apples, unpeeled, cored
    and sliced into wedges**
85 ml/5½ tbsp water
**1–2 tbsp honey or maple syrup,
    to taste**

Makes 4-6 servings

*Apple purée is a staple in our house. We use it as an
accompaniment to yogurt and porridge and as a baking
ingredient to add moisture in place of eggs at times, but
its crowning glory is the contribution it can make to improve
digestion thanks, in part, to its pectin content.*

Put all of the ingredients into the Instant Pot. Set to PRESSURE
for 2 minutes. NPR at the end and process in a food processor
once cool enough.

Leave to cool further then store in a sealable container in the
fridge and use as required.

WINE-POACHED FIGS ⓥ

250 g/9 oz. fresh figs
250 ml/1 cup red wine (vegan,
    if preferred)
¾ tsp ground cinnamon
1 tsp vanilla extract
50 g/3½ tbsp caster/superfine
    sugar
double/heavy cream or Vegan
    Cream (see page 11), to serve

Serves 2

*A simple recipe with great results.
The red wine syrup poured over the
pressure-cooked figs makes for
a delicious dinner-party dessert.*

Put the figs in the Instant Pot steaming basket.
Stir the wine, cinnamon, vanilla and sugar in the
Instant Pot. Put the trivet on top then pop the
steaming basket with the figs in on top. Set to
PRESSURE for 2 minutes then QPR at the end
of cooking. Remove the steaming basket and
trivet and set aside. Press SAUTÉ and stir
occasionally for about 5 minutes until the sauce
has reduced and thickened to a syrup.

Serve with a dollop of cream or Vegan
Cream, as preferred.

COCONUT FLOUR BANANA CAKE

3–4 VERY ripe bananas (about 300 g/10½ oz.), plus extra sliced banana, to serve
1 tbsp smooth almond butter
4 eggs
2 tbsp honey or maple syrup, plus extra to serve
30 g/2 tbsp oil
1 tsp vanilla extract
70 g/⅔ cup coconut flour
1 tsp bicarbonate of soda/baking soda
pinch of salt
coconut cream, to serve (optional)

15-cm/6-inch diameter springform baking pan

Serves 6–8

Coconut flour is naturally gluten free, high in fibre and low in carbohydrates. In this moist banana cake, it provides a mild coconut flavour that contrasts nicely with the other ingredients.

Mash the bananas in a large bowl then add all other wet ingredients i.e. almond butter, eggs, honey or maple syrup, oil and vanilla. In another bowl mix the dry ingredients i.e. the coconut flour, bicarbonate of soda/baking soda and salt. Combine the mixtures in the largest bowl and stir. Pour the mixture into the baking pan. Pour 500 ml/2 cups water into the Instant Pot. Add the trivet. Place the filled cake pan on top. Cook at PRESSURE for 30 minutes then NPR at the end of cooking. Leave to cool before slicing.

Serve with a dollop of coconut cream, sliced banana and a drizzle of honey or maple syrup, if liked.

CARROT & ORANGE LOAF CAKE

1 small carrot, grated (85 g/scant ¾ cup once grated)
2 eggs
½ tsp vanilla extract
6 drops food-grade orange oil
75 g/6 tbsp brown sugar or coconut sugar
110 g/heaped 1 cup ground almonds
1 tsp baking powder
½ tsp each ground ginger and ground cinnamon
pinch of salt
crème fraîche, to serve (optional)

15 x 8 x 5-cm/6 x 3¼ x 2-inch small loaf pan, greased

Serves 4

This is a deliciously moist grain-free cake. The carrot and orange combination brings fresh, zingy taste to this dessert.

In a food processor combine all ingredients and put in the prepared loaf pan. Place 500 ml/2 cups water into the Instant Pot. Place the trivet on top and the filled loaf pan on top of the trivet. Set to PRESSURE for 16 minutes and allow an NPR at the end of cooking. Lift the lid and leave to cool before slicing.

Serve with a dollop of crème fraîche, if liked.

GINGER & PISTACHIO CHIA RICE PUDDING

1 tbsp butter
200 g/2 cups pudding
   (short-grain) rice
1 heaped tbsp chia seeds
1.4 litres/6 cups any milk of your
   choice
85 g/3 oz. stem ginger, very
   finely chopped
2 tbsp maple syrup
100 g/1 cup chopped unsalted
   pistachios, to serve

Serves 8

This is a rich and creamy tasting rice pudding with a classic flavour combination of ginger and pistachio.

Set the Instant Pot to SAUTÉ and add the butter. Once melted add the rice and chia seeds, and stir to coat. Add the milk and still on SAUTÉ bring to the boil. Add the ginger and maple syrup, and stir again. Cover with the lid and set to PRESSURE for 12 minutes, then NPR at the end of cooking. Remove the lid and stir.

Serve warm with the pistachios over the top.

BROWN RICE PUDDING ⓥ

100 g/1 cup brown rice
380 ml/1½ cups plant-based milk
1 tsp vanilla extract
½ tsp ground cinnamon, plus
   extra to serve
1 tbsp maple syrup
125 ml/½ cup coconut cream

Serves 2–3

Whilst rice pudding is a popular dessert some would like a slightly healthier version, and this is just that. It's made with wholegrain rice and lower sugar levels than a traditional rice pudding. This is also a plant-based rice pudding suitable for vegans.

Put all ingredients except the coconut cream into the Instant Pot, stir well then cook at PRESSURE for 25 minutes with NPR for 10 minutes. Release the remaining pressure then stir in the coconut cream.

Serve warm with a dusting of cinnamon, if liked.

MOLASSES FLAPJACK Ⓥ

120 g/8½ tbsp butter or vegan
   spread
90 g/scant ½ cup sugar
40 g/2 tbsp blackstrap molasses
   or black treacle
225 g/2⅓ cups rolled/
   old-fashioned oats

15-cm/6-inch diameter
   springform baking pan,
   greased

Serves 6–8

*This is a wholesome flapjack, slightly darker in colour
thanks to the iron-rich molasses used to flavour.*

Heat the Instant Pot on SAUTÉ. Add the butter or spread,
sugar and molasses and stir for about 2 minutes until
completely melted. Stir in the oats then press CANCEL.

   Push the oat mixture into the prepared baking pan using
the back of a spoon.

   Place 500 ml/2 cups water in the Instant Pot, set the
trivet on top then lower the filled baking pan on top. Set to
20 minutes at PRESSURE. NPR at the end of cooking.

   Leave to cool completely before carefully removing and
slicing into portions to serve.

CHOCOLATE CRANBERRY TIFFIN

120 g/4 oz. dark chocolate
130 g/generous ½ cup Apple
   Purée (see page 125)
2 medium eggs
1 tsp vanilla extract
1 tbsp oil
pinch of salt
2½ tbsp arrowroot powder
2 tbsp raw cacao powder, plus
   extra to serve
40 g/scant ⅓ cup dried,
   sweetened cranberries
70 g/1 cup digestive biscuit/
   Graham cracker pieces

15-cm/6-inch diameter
   springform baking pan,
   greased and lined

Serves 6–8

*This favourite sweet treat from my childhood has
received the 'upgrade' it deserved from a health
perspective. I've reduced the sugars and increased the
antioxidants available so that I can justify enjoying it
on a regular basis!*

Put the chocolate in a covered bowl on the trivet of the Instant
Pot and add 250 ml/1 cup water. Set to SAUTÉ and heat until
the water is bubbling slightly and the chocolate melted. In
a large bowl, mix the melted chocolate with the remaining
ingredients, adding in the order listed. Stir the biscuit/cracker
pieces in gently so they don't break up too much. Pour the
mixture into the prepared baking pan. Place the trivet into the
Instant Pot with 500 ml/2 cups water below. Place the pan on
top. Set to PRESSURE for 8 minutes. Use QPR at the end of
cooking. Allow to cool a little then remove from the pan.

   Transfer to the fridge to cool completely before dusting
with cacao powder and slicing into portions to serve.

LITTLE APRICOT CRUMBLES ⓥ

1 x 400-g/14-oz. can apricot
    halves in fruit juice
50 g/½ cup rolled/old-fashioned
    oats
50 g/½ cup almond flour/ground
    almonds
10 g/2 tsp chia seeds
¾ tsp ground cinnamon
15 g/1 tbsp brown sugar or
    coconut sugar
50 g/2½ tbsp coconut oil, melted

4 x individual ramekins (that fit
    into your Instant Pot when on
    the trivet)

Serves 4

*These individual crumbles take just minutes to prepare
and then can be left to cook. As pressure is released
naturally you can come back to these when dessert
time comes without having to go into the kitchen to
prepare something from scratch.*

Place 5–6 apricot halves in each ramekin. Drain a little but
keep about 2 tsp of juice in each ramekin as this helps keep
the crumbles moist. In a bowl mix the oats, almond flour/
ground almonds, chia seeds, cinnamon, sugar and
coconut oil.
    Drop an equal amount of the crumble mixture on top
of each filled ramekin. Place 500 ml/2 cups water in
the Instant Pot then put the trivet on top and the filled
ramekins on top of that. Cook for 10 minutes at PRESSURE
and allow an NPR before serving.

APPLE CRUMBLE ⓥ

6 eating apples, unpeeled, cored
    and cut into wedges
50 ml/3½ tbsp water
1 tsp maple syrup
½ tsp ground cinnamon
¼ tsp ground ginger
4 tbsp melted butter or
    coconut oil
75 g/¾ cup rolled/old-fashioned
    oats
25 g/3 tbsp gluten-free plain/
    all-purpose flour
30 g/2½ tbsp brown sugar
pinch of salt

Serves 3–4

*This is a quick and simple one pot crumble. The
base is fibre, and pectin-rich apples and the topping
which is scattered over the cooked apple tastes like
a disassembled flapjack. Yummy!*

Place the apples on the bottom of the Instant Pot. Stir in
the water and maple syrup then sprinkle over the spices.
Mix the melted butter or coconut oil with the oats, flour,
sugar and salt. Drop the crumble mixture by the spoonful
on top of the apples. Secure the lid on the Instant Pot.
Cook at the PRESSURE for 1 minute and allow an NPR
before serving.

4 ripe nectarines, sliced into
    quarters and stoned/pitted
150 g/heaped 1 cup frozen
    raspberries
2 tbsp honey
190 g/scant 1½ cups plain/
    all-purpose flour
3 tbsp sugar
1 tsp baking powder
¾ tsp ground cinnamon
½ tsp ground ginger
3 tbsp coconut oil, melted
40 ml/2½ tbsp milk
1 egg, beaten
crème fraîche, to serve (optional)

Serves 4

MELBA COBBLER

A delightful combination of nectarines and raspberries
combined with some spice, oats and honey.

Mix the nectarines, raspberries and honey in a heatproof, suitably
sized bowl for PIP cooking in the Instant Pot.

In a separate bowl mix together the flour, sugar, baking powder,
spices, melted coconut oil, milk and egg.

Spread the cobbler mixture over the fruit in the bowl then pop
the pot on the trivet in the Instant Pot with 500 ml/2 cups water
below. Set to PRESSURE for 10 minutes and allow an NPR at the
end of cooking.

Serve with a dollop of crème fraîche on top of each serving,
if liked.

120 ml/½ cup oil
2 eggs
90 g/⅓ cup Apple Purée (see
    page 125)
1 eating apple, unpeeled and
    grated
150 g/1 cup plus 2 tbsp
    self-raising/rising flour
100 g/½ cup unrefined sugar
1 tsp baking powder
1 tsp ground cinnamon
any cream, to serve (optional)

15-cm/6-inch diameter
    springform baking pan,
    greased

Serves 6–8

APPLE & CINNAMON SPONGE

Here is a light sponge with a winning apple and cinnamon
combination. The apple purée/applesauce can be shop-bought
or made from the recipe on page 125, as preferred.

In a bowl mix together the wet ingredients then add the dry
ingredients. Mix everything together then pour into the prepared
pan. Put 500 ml/2 cups water into the Instant Pot and place the
trivet on top then the filled cake pan on top of that. Set to
PRESSURE for 35 minutes then NPR for 15 minutes before releasing
the pressure. Dab any excess water off
the surface then allow to cool
for about 10 minutes
before serving with
cream, if liked.

OLIVE OIL CHOCOLATE CAKE Ⓥ

75 g/½ cup plus 1 tbsp plain/
    all-purpose flour
80 g/generous ⅓ cup brown
    sugar/coconut sugar
20 g/2 tbsp raw cacao powder,
    plus extra to serve
½ tsp baking powder
½ tsp bicarbonate of soda/
    baking soda
pinch of salt
125 ml/½ cup oat milk
60 ml/4 tbsp extra virgin olive oil
½ tsp vanilla extract
1 tsp apple cider vinegar
Vegan Cream (see page 11),
    to serve (optional)

15-cm/6-inch diameter
    springform baking pan,
    greased and lined

Serves 6–8

This is a torte-like vegan cake. Ideal for serving at the end of a special meal with a dollop of Vegan Cream.

In a bowl mix the flour, sugar, cacao powder, baking powder, bicarbonate of soda/baking soda and salt. In a separate bowl whisk together the oat milk, oil, vanilla and apple cider vinegar. Combine the two mixtures in the largest of the bowls. Pour the mixture into the prepared baking pan. Put 500 ml/2 cups water in the Instant Pot. Pop the trivet then the filled cake pan on top. Set to PRESSURE for 35 minutes then QPR for 15 minutes. Remove the lid, press CANCEL then allow the cake to cool a little before removing from the pot, then the cake pan.

Slice into portions, dust with cacao powder and serve with a good dollop of Vegan Cream, if liked.

RAW CHOCOLATE BROWNIES Ⓥ

reserved almond pulp from
    1 x recipe Almond Milk (see
    page 141)
170 g/1¼ cups pitted dates
30 g/2 rounded tbsp raw cacao
    powder, plus extra to finish
pinch of salt
4 drops food-grade orange oil

Serves 4

When you make my recipe for Almond Milk (see page 141) what to do with the leftover almond pulp? Here is the best way to use it up... by making vegan chocolate brownies! (See a photograph on page 140.)

Place all ingredients into a food processor and blitz until combined.

Use damp hands to roll the mixture into walnut-sized balls. Roll these in a little extra cacao powder, if liked. Arrange the balls on a plate or tray, and cover and refrigerate until ready to enjoy.

ALMOND MILK ⓥ

140 g/1 heaped cup whole
   almonds
250 ml/1 cup water for cooking
   plus 1 litre/4 cups for blending
1 tsp vanilla extract
1 tbsp maple syrup

Serves 4

*When you make almond milk from scratch most recipes
will tell you soak the almonds overnight, but if you want
even faster results then pressure cooking your almonds
will bring the outcome you're looking for. They make for
a creamy, delicious plant-based milk.*

Place the almonds and 250 ml/1 cup water in the Instant Pot
and set to PRESSURE for 3 minutes. QPR at the end of
cooking. Drain and rinse the almonds then place into a blender
or food processor with 1 litre/4 cups water, the vanilla extract
and maple syrup. Process until the mixture is frothy and the
almonds all blended. Pass the contents of the blender/
processor through some muslin/cheesecloth or a nut milk bag.
(Reserve these to make the Raw Chocolate Brownies on page
138, if liked.)

   Store the almond milk in a sealable container into the
fridge and use as required.

COCONUT CHAI LATTE ⓥ

1 tbsp fresh turmeric root, grated
   (do this with gloves on as the
   orange can stain your hands)
1 tbsp grated fresh ginger
3 whole cardamom pods
2 whole cinnamon sticks
6 whole black peppercorns
750 ml/3 cups water
1 x 400-ml/14-oz. can coconut
   milk
2–3 tbsp maple syrup, to taste
1 tsp vanilla extract

Serves 6–8

*At the end of a meal you may want something soothing
and warming to ease digestion. This combination of spices
– turmeric, ginger, pepper, cardamom and cinnamon –
once combined with creamy coconut milk makes for an
ideal end-of-meal drink without any caffeine.*

Place the spices and water in the Instant Pot and set to
PRESSURE for 5 minutes. NPR at the end of cooking then
separate the liquid from the spices using a sieve/strainer.
Reserve the liquid. Place the coconut milk into the Instant Pot
and set to SAUTÉ. Stirring with a whisk, add the maple syrup,
vanilla extract and reserved spiced water until heated through.
   Serve immediately, poured into heatproof glasses or cups.

INDEX

A

almond milk 141
amino acids 9–10
apples: apple & cinnamon
    sponge 137
  apple crumble 134
  apple purée 125
  spiced apple porridge 15
apricot crumbles 134
asparagus: creamy
  asparagus soup 29
aubergine, tomato &
  potato curry 57

B

bananas: choco-nana
  quinoa porridge 16
  coconut flour banana
  cake 129
beans: soaking 9
  see also green beans,
  mung beans etc
beetroot, perfect 109
black beans: black bean
  chilli 61
  black beans & rice 61
  Mexican black bean &
  chocolate chilli 61
  Mexican spicy rice 113
bolognese, vegan tempeh
  85
broad/fava beans:
  Middle Eastern fava
  bean stew 39
butternut squash: black
  bean chilli 61
  butternut squash &
  green bean dhal 23
  Middle Eastern fava
  bean stew 39
  pasta with butternut
  squash & sage sauce 89

C

cakes 129, 137–8
compôte, 'baked' 99
carrots: carrot & green
  bean curry 46
  carrot & leek risotto 72
  carrot & orange loaf
  cake 129
  fennel & carrot soup 34
  spinach, carrot, chickpea
  & lemon pilaff 75
cashews: vegan cream 11
  vegan sour cream 11
cauliflower: cauliflower &
  potato curry 45
  cauliflower cheese soup 95

cauliflower masala 45
classic cauliflower cheese
  95
chai & turmeric porridge 19
chana dal, kitchari 24
cheese: 'baked'
  Camembert 99
  Brie & cider risotto 103
  cauliflower cheese soup
  95
  cheesy enchilada rice
  soup 96
  classic cauliflower cheese
  95
  creamy cheese & spinach
  pasta 89
  Emmental, red pepper &
  tomato crustless
  quiches 98
  fennel & feta risotto 72
  feta, pea & mint crustless
  quiches 98
  halloumi, chickpea &
  spinach curry 49
  halloumi, chickpeas &
  preserved lemons 103
  leek & Caerphilly cheese
  soup 96
  leek, pea & halloumi
  quinotto 80
  Mediterranean goats'
  cheese, lentil & sweet
  potato pies 104
  Mediterranean rice with
  halloumi 76
  quinoa tabbouleh with
  feta 80
chia seeds: ginger &
  pistachio chia rice
  pudding 130
  strawberry chia compôte
  125
chickpeas: chickpea &
  potato curry 57
  chickpea, potato &
  tomato saffron stew 40
  halloumi, chickpea &
  spinach curry 49
  halloumi, chickpeas &
  preserved lemons 103
  red pepper hummus 118
  spinach, carrot, chickpea
  & lemon pilaff 75
  sweet potato & chickpea
  satay curry 54
chilli: black bean chilli 61
  Mexican black bean &
  chocolate chilli 61
  smoky pinto bean chilli
  58
chocolate: choco-nana
  quinoa porridge 16

chocolate cranberry tiffin
  133
  Mexican black bean &
  chocolate chilli 61
  olive oil chocolate cake
  138
  raw chocolate brownies
  138
chowder, sweetcorn 34
coconut chai latte 141
coconut flour banana cake
  129
courgettes/zucchini:
  courgette & pesto soup
  30
  spaghetti with courgette
  & lemon 87
couscous, wholewheat 117
cranberries: chocolate
  cranberry tiffin 133
cream: vegan cream 11
  vegan sour cream 11
curry: aubergine, tomato &
  potato curry 57
  carrot & green bean curry
  46
  cauliflower & potato curry
  45
  cauliflower masala 45
  chickpea & potato curry
  57
  creamy vegetarian
  kedgeree 79
  green Thai tofu curry 53
  halloumi, chickpea &
  spinach curry 49
  Indonesian lentil curry 54
  quick mild vegetable
  curry 46
  red Thai vegetable curry
  53
  sweet potato & chickpea
  satay curry 54
  tofu massaman 49
  vegetable korma 50

D E

dhal: butternut squash &
  green bean dhal 23
  creamy mung bean dhal
  23
  simple red lentil dhal 24
eggs 9
  creamy vegetarian
  kedgeree 79
  egg-fried vegetable
  brown rice 76
  Emmental, red pepper &
  tomato crustless
  quiches 98
  feta, pea & mint crustless
  quiches 98

perfect soft-boiled eggs
  99

F

fats 8
fava bean stew, Middle
  Eastern 39
fennel: fennel & carrot
  soup 34
  fennel & feta risotto 72
figs, wine poached 126
flapjack, molasses 133

G H

garlic: garlic mushroom
  pasta 90
  garlic, spinach &
  mushroom brown rice
  68
ginger & pistachio chia rice
  pudding 130
grains 9
gram flour pancakes 50
Greek split yellow pea &
  garlic purée 118
green beans: butternut
  squash & green bean dhal
  23
  carrot & green bean curry
  46
  perfect green beans 110
  green herb risotto 71
  green Thai tofu curry 53
haricot/navy beans:
  homemade baked beans
  114
harissa, red pepper &
  tomato soup 33
hummus, red pepper 118

I J

Indonesian lentil curry 54
jackfruit, pulled BBQ 36

K L

kale: green herb risotto 71
kedgeree, creamy
  vegetarian 79
kitchari 24
korma, vegetable 50
latte, coconut chai 141
leeks: carrot & leek risotto
  72
  leek & Caerphilly cheese
  soup 96
  leek & mushroom risotto
  68
  leek, pea & halloumi
  quinotto 80
  savoury leek porridge 20
lentils: butternut squash &
  green bean dhal 23

Indonesian lentil curry 54
Mediterranean goats'
   cheese, lentil & sweet
   potato pies 104
Mediterranean lentil stew
   40
Moroccan lentil stew 39
simple red lentil dhal 24
sun-blushed tomato &
   lentil pasta 90
lettuce: summer greens
   soup 29

M
mango quinoa breakfast
   bowl 16
Mediterranean goats'
   cheese, lentil & sweet
   potato pies 104
Mediterranean lentil stew
   40
Mediterranean rice with
   halloumi 76
Melba cobbler 137
Mexican black bean &
   chocolate chilli 61
Mexican spicy rice 113
Middle Eastern fava bean
   stew 39
milk, almond 141
molasses flapjack 133
Moroccan lentil stew 39
mung bean dhal 23
mushrooms: Brie & cider
   risotto 103
   garlic mushroom pasta 90
   garlic, spinach &
      mushroom brown rice 68
   leek & mushroom risotto
      68
   savoury mushroom & pea
      porridge 20
   vegan mushroom risotto
      67
   vegan tempeh bolognese
      85

N O
nectarines: Melba cobbler
   137
oats: apple crumble 134
   little apricot crumbles
      134
   molasses flapjack 133
   see also porridge
oils 8
olive oil chocolate cake 138

P
paella, vegetable 75
pancakes, gram flour 50
pasta 10

3-ingredient tomato
   pasta 87
creamy cheese & spinach
   pasta 89
garlic mushroom pasta
   90
pasta with butternut
   squash & sage sauce 89
spaghetti with courgette
   & lemon 87
sun-blushed tomato &
   lentil pasta 90
vegan tempeh bolognese
   85
vegan veggie pasta 85
peas: feta, pea & mint
   crustless quiches 98
   mushy peas 110
   savoury mushroom & pea
      porridge 20
   summer greens soup 29
peppers (bell): Emmental,
   red pepper & tomato
   crustless quiches 98
   harissa, red pepper &
      tomato soup 33
   red pepper hummus 118
   vegan veggie pasta 85
pesto: courgette & pesto
   soup 30
pies: Mediterranean goats'
   cheese, lentil & sweet
   potato 104
pilaff: spinach, carrot,
   chickpea & lemon pilaff
   75
   vegetable pilaff 120
pinto beans: pulled BBQ
   jackfruit with pinto beans
   36
   refried beans 113
   smoky pinto bean chilli
      58
pistachio nuts: ginger &
   pistachio chia rice
   pudding 130
porridge: chai & turmeric
   porridge 19
   choco-nana quinoa
      porridge 16
   quinoa & oat savoury
      porridge 19
   savoury leek porridge 20
   savoury mushroom & pea
      porridge 20
   simple pot-in-pot
      porridge 15
   spiced apple porridge 15
potatoes: aubergine,
   tomato & potato curry 57
   cauliflower & potato curry
      45

chickpea & potato curry
   57
chickpea, potato &
   tomato saffron stew 40
creamy asparagus soup
   29
creamy mashed potatoes
   114
vegan sausage & potato
   stew 36
proteins, combining 9–10

Q R
quiches, crustless 98
quinoa: choco-nana
   quinoa porridge 16
   leek, pea & halloumi
      quinotto 80
   mango quinoa breakfast
      bowl 16
   quinoa & oat savoury
      porridge 19
   quinoa tabbouleh with
      feta 80
raspberries: Melba cobbler
   137
ratatouille, instant 117
refried beans 113
rhubarb compôte 125
rice: black beans & rice 61
   brown rice pudding 130
   'buttery' brown basmati
      rice 120
   cheesy enchilada rice
      soup 96
   creamy vegetarian
      kedgeree 79
   egg-fried vegetable
      brown rice 76
   garlic, spinach &
      mushroom brown rice 68
   ginger & pistachio chia
      rice pudding 130
   kitchari 24
   Mediterranean rice with
      halloumi 76
   Mexican spicy rice 113
   vegetable paella 75
   see also pilaff; risotto
risotto: Brie & cider risotto
   103
   carrot & leek risotto 72
   fennel & feta risotto 72
   fresh tomato risotto 71
   green herb risotto 71
   leek & mushroom risotto
      68
   vegan mushroom risotto
      67

S
sausage & potato stew 36

soups 29–35, 95–7
sour cream, vegan 11
spaghetti with courgette &
   lemon 87
spinach: creamy cheese &
   spinach pasta 89
   garlic, spinach &
      mushroom brown rice 68
   halloumi, chickpea &
      spinach curry 49
   halloumi, chickpeas &
      preserved lemons 103
   spinach, carrot, chickpea
      & lemon pilaff 75
stews 36–41
strawberry chia compôte
   125
sugars 9
summer greens soup 29
sweet potatoes:
   Mediterranean goats'
   cheese, lentil & sweet
   potato pies 104
   sweet potato & chickpea
      satay curry 54
sweetcorn chowder 34

T
tabbouleh, quinoa 80
tempeh bolognese 85
tofu: green Thai tofu curry
   53
   tofu massaman 49
tomatoes: 3-ingredient
   tomato pasta 87
   aubergine, tomato &
      potato curry 57
   Emmental, red pepper &
      tomato crustless
      quiches 98
   fresh tomato risotto 71
   fresh tomato soup 33
   harissa, red pepper &
      tomato soup 33
   homemade baked beans
      114
   sun-blushed tomato &
      lentil pasta 90
   vegan veggie pasta 85

V Y
vegetables: instant
   ratatouille 117
   quick mild vegetable
      curry 46
   red Thai vegetable curry 53
   vegetable korma 50
   vegetable paella 75
   vegetable pilaff 120
yellow split peas: Greek
   split yellow pea & garlic
   purée 118

ACKNOWLEDGEMENTS

I have to start by thanking my publishers Ryland, Peters & Small. Special thanks go to Julia Charles for editorial direction and in particular for compiling the categories for this book. Also thanks to Cindy Richards, who as Publisher has helped in bringing the book together into a beautiful collection we can all be proud of, Leslie Harrington for art direction and design, and Patricia Harrington, Head of Production. Thanks also go to photographer Clare Winfield for creating the wonderful images that accompany these carefully created recipes, along with Food Stylist Emily Kydd and Prop Stylist Olivia Wardle. Thank you once again to my fantastic literary agent Jane Graham-Maw who continues to champion my work. To my recipe testers Sue Crane, Vicky Everitt, Anna Hemmings MBE, Soyen Adams, Malissa Berry, Carolyn Davenport, Michelle Brown, Abi Ricketts, Vanessa Hill and Tina Foote thank you. Many of you are relatively new to the Instant Pot® and having your frank and honest input has been an incredibly important part of the creative process. To my family and friends for being chief tasters and for supporting and entertaining me during those long hours spent in the kitchen developing and testing new recipes.

Jenny Tschiesche
BSc(Hons) Dip(ION) FdSc BANT